DIE, MOMMIE, DIE! *and* PSYCHO BEACH PARTY
The Screenplays of Charles Busch

DIE, MOMMIE, DIE!
and
PSYCHO BEACH PARTY

The Screenplays
of Charles Busch

with an introduction
by Charles Busch

alyson books
NEW YORK

Manufactured in the United States of America

An original trade paperback published by Alyson Books
245 West 17th Street, New York, NY 10011

Distribution in the United Kingdom by Turnaround Publisher Services Ltd.
Unit 3, Olympia Trading Estate, Coburg Road, Wood Green
London N22 6TZ England

First Edition: February 2008

08 09 10 11 12 **a** 10 9 8 7 6 5 4 3 2 1

ISBN: 1-59350-025-4
ISBN-13: 978-1-59350-025-2

Cover design by Victor Mingovits.

CONTENTS

INTRODUCTION

I have always loved the movies. I think the first film I saw in a theatre was *Gone With the Wind*. No, my dears, not in its original release. It must have been a 1961 reissue. And although I was not more than a toddler, I can still remember being enchanted by the rich Technicolor photography and the extraordinary image of Scarlett dragging the horse and wagon underneath the bridge in the rain.

My father adored the movies, and I used to stay up until two in the morning nearly every night with him watching "The Late Show," "Movie Greats," and "Million Dollar Movie." My father had a very romantic sensibility, and he loved movies such as *Random Harvest* and *Casablanca*. I assimilated so much movie trivia that by the age of ten I could recite the list of every female Oscar winner from 1927 on. One of the reasons I got away with staying up so late was that my mother died when I was seven. My father was very loving, but not the most responsible of parents. With his blessing, I was ultimately raised by my Aunt Lillian, who swept me out of the suburbs to live with her in Manhattan. Is it any wonder that the novel, play, and movie of *Auntie Mame* have been an integral part of my life? Aunt Lillian was a widow with no children and very much like the noble and indomitable women that Ida Lupino, Barbara Stanwyck, and Bette Davis used to play. I was very aware of her painful battles with the trustees of my uncle's estate and her fierce desire to protect my sisters and me.

When I was ten years old, the movie *Hush . . . Hush, Sweet Charlotte* opened, and I dragged Aunt Lillian all the way up to the Bronx to see it, because I read in the newspaper that Bette Davis and Olivia de Havilland were going to make a personal appearance. Indeed they did. After the movie they strode onto the stage and conducted a very lively Q and A with the audience. Both ladies exuded such confidence, authority, and great humor. Perhaps that was when I began in earnest my lifelong infatuation with actresses.

Years later in college at Northwestern University, I began writing roles for myself. And from the very beginning they were female. I never wanted to be a woman, but I desperately wanted to be an actress. Somehow, young male roles seemed impossibly dreary. Wouldn't anyone rather play Blanche DuBois than Willy Loman's son Biff? I became a writer to give myself opportunities to act. Surprisingly, I never intellectualized why it was I only wanted to play female characters – it just seemed the natural way to express myself. Perhaps I was afraid that any deep self-reflection would tell me things about myself I wasn't ready to hear.

In the mid-1980s, I helped create a theatre company known as Theatre-in-Limbo. We began performing in a very kooky art gallery/ performance space/after-hours bar deep in the farthest reaches of Manhattan's (at-that-time) undeveloped East Village. We quickly developed a cult following, mounting plays with titles such as *Vampire Lesbians of Sodom; Theodora, She-Bitch of Byzantium;* and *Pardon My Inquisition, or Kiss the Blood Off My Castanets*. We transferred the most outrageous of these pieces, *Vampire Lesbians of Sodom*, to a commercial run Off Broadway that ran a record-breaking five years. We did other plays as well, such as *The Lady in Question, Red Scare on Sunset*, and one of our most successful works, *Psycho Beach Party*, which was originally titled *Gidget Goes Psychotic*. All of these plays starred me as the leading lady and were inspired by old movies.

When I finally made my movie debut in 1992 with a small role in *Addams Family Values*, I was so overcome with emotion that when the director called action, I actually fainted right in front of the film's star, Angelica Huston. I played a few small roles in movies and TV, but mostly ended up on the cutting room floor. As I had done in the theatre, I had to wait till one of my own plays was made into a movie for me to have a sizeable film role. That finally happened just as the century was about to turn. My great friend and manager, Jeff Melnick, kept insisting that my play *Psycho Beach Party* would make a terrific movie. Frankly I didn't see it. It was a very stylized theatrical piece that combined two very different movie genres: the beach party movies of the sixties and Hitchcock suspense films, notably *Marnie*. Jeff pursued this for eight years. Every once in a while he would tell me which movie company had passed. Finally in 2000 he teamed me up with one of his directing clients, Robert Lee King, and convinced Strand Releasing to produce the movie. Jeff's tenacity led me to joke that *Psycho Beach Party* was Jeff's *Gandhi* (another little movie that took many years to come to fruition).

I had never written a screenplay, and was very fortunate to have as my director an experienced screenwriter. It was Bob King's idea to make the movie more of a thriller. In the play, the only crime that's committed is that some unknown psychopath is drugging the young surfers and shaving their bodies head to toe; a whimsical and not very terrifying crime. Bob thought we needed to up the stakes a tad. So in the film we added the character of a true serial killer on the loose.

The producers of the movie wanted me to write a role for myself. It was deemed by all, myself included, that I should not play my original role of the teenage Chicklet. I didn't think any camera could accommodate that many filters. We were thrilled to find a young actress named Lauren Ambrose to be our star. (She has since found fame on the television series *Six Feet Under* and on the stage.) But the great, agonizing question was: Who would I play? I thought briefly of taking on the role of the Joan Crawford-esque mother, but that was too obvious. I've always been very selective about which roles in my plays and movies should be cross-dressed. I prefer to have the flamboyant female roles played by real women and save the drag role for a less obvious choice. Which role would I play? Well, I thought, if we have a killer on the loose, then we need to have a sleuth. Why could I not play a tough-though-terribly-chic lady police detective? And so, Captain Monica Stark was born. The costume designer took me to a costume rental house to find me a uniform. I tried on several traditional policewoman uniforms, and never have I looked more masculine in my life. I saw the character as Susan Hayward, in her mature *Valley of the Dolls* persona. I suggested that we look for a highly tailored flight-attendant uniform. We found the perfect one on the racks and, with a little bit of altering and a great pair of not-quite-police-regulation spike heels, I was ready for action.

It was so thrilling to walk on the various sets, such as the movie star's beach house and Kanaka's shack. Although it was a very low-budget film, it still seemed like a large production to me. I couldn't believe that all of this activity and creativity was being expended because of some idle fantasy of mine.

A few months before I flew to Los Angeles to film *Psycho Beach Party*, my friend Ken Elliott phoned me. He was the original stage director of so many of my plays including *Vampire Lesbians of Sodom* and *Psycho Beach Party*. Ken was living in Los Angeles by this time and suggested that we do a play together while I was in town. This may sound kind of kooky, but this was the way we always operated. Writing and putting on a play was not a complicated deal full of artistic agonizing – it was more akin to planning a party. It was a swell idea, partly because I knew that my role in the movie of *Psycho Beach Party* would take only a few days of shooting, and I thought it would keep me out of Bob King's hair. Directors have a funny way of wanting the screenwriter to be available twenty-four hours a day but silent as cloistered nuns. I was at a loss for an idea for a play and thought, maybe, there was a story from the classics that would give me the germ of a plot. My first idea was to do an update of Oedipus, with myself as the glamorous mother, Jocasta. The more I worked on it, the more I realized that that the play was called "Oedipus the King" for a good reason. Oedipus remains front and center while his old ma stands in the background wringing her hands and dies at the top of Act Two. All ego aside, I wanted this to be a fabulous starring vehicle for ME. Then my dear friend Carl Andress, who was going to join me in Los Angeles to perform in this as yet non-existent vehicle, suggested the myth of the house of Atreus. Clytemnestra! Now *that* was a gal with a lot of style and gumption, I thought the story of an adulterous queen who murders her powerful husband and whose son and daughter are obsessed with her guilt would be the makings of a hilarious screen comedy. It immediately occurred to me that I should set it in the 1960s and have it be an homage to a film genre sometimes known as "Grande Dame Guignol." These were movies such as *Whatever Happened to Baby Jane, Dead Ringer, Hush . . . Hush, Sweet Charlotte, Die! Die! My Darling!, Picture Mommy Dead*, and *Strait-Jacket*, which gave somewhat questionable employment to a whole raft of aging Hollywood actresses during the 1960s.

We rehearsed the play, which was now called *Die, Mommie, Die!*, while *Psycho Beach Party* was being filmed. As bad luck would have it, I was called to film on the day of our opening night. We were shooting a scene where Captain Monica Stark first meets Chicklet. It was shot all the way up in what is known as Canyon Country, a good two hours outside of L.A. As is usual on a movie set, hours can go by in preparation with lights being set up, and we didn't begin shooting the scene until after 4 o'clock in the afternoon. It became clear I would not make the 8 o'clock curtain and I felt horribly guilty that I had let down the cast of *Die, Mommie, Die!* I had no understudy. While I was making that dreaded phone call to the stage manager, *Psycho Beach Party*'s director, Bob King, whispered to me, "You better tell them that you won't be there for their next two performances either." Our opening night was pushed to the following week and we quickly sold out the small Coast Theater in West Hollywood for the next few months.

While I was doing the play, it occurred to me that *Die, Mommie, Die!* would make an excellent small indie film. After all, the entire play took place in one house and I was learning that a small number of locations in a movie translated into fewer days filming and that meant a lower budget. I believe I began writing the screenplay while I was still performing the play. It was great being able to apply some of the lessons that I had just learned from adapting *Psycho Beach Party* to the screen.

Whereas *Psycho Beach Party* took eight years to come to fruition, *Die, Mommie, Die!* began filming within a year. The crazy nineteen-day shooting schedule of *Die, Mommie, Die!* was perhaps the most exciting three weeks of my life. This was the first time I was actually starring in a movie, and as I began filming every scene, I couldn't believe my great fortune. I was truly living out my most outrageous fantasies. We had a great cast, including Jason Priestley, Philip Baker Hall, Natasha Lyonne, Stark Sands, and, once again, an alumna from *Six Feet Under*, Frances Conroy.

For so many years, I had been playing these inspiring movie heroines who evoked Bette Davis, Joan Crawford, and Rosalind Russell, and in the theatre I had to exaggerate their acting style to project to the last row. In a movie, I could more accurately recreate their acting style. These film stars were, after all, essentially film actresses. I didn't want to be doing an actual impersonation, because Angela Arden had to be a believable character with her own voice and mannerisms. I found myself intellectually playing a scene in the manner of Bette Davis, rather than using her patented clipped consonants and body language.

This was Mark Rucker's first film as a director. He's had a wonderful career in the theatre and came to this production extraordinarily well prepared. Filming went remarkably smoothly. Some days we actually shot more than was planned. Only on one day was there a disaster: All the generators shut down and an underwater camera broke. Shooting stopped for several hours, which is disastrous on a low-budget film. Everyone was demoralized and tense. Finally, when the technical problems were ironed out, we shot an important scene where Angela performs at her husband's memorial service. I had a scene where I had to sing three separate songs with the pianist. From what I hear, many screen actors don't really enjoy performing in front of an audience and prefer to do these scenes without an actual audience of extras. Not this hambone. Instead of performing brief portions of the songs, I sang the entire numbers and put on quite a show for the cast and crew. Frankly, I had a marvelous time cutting loose. Later, I was told it really helped bring back the company's spirits.

One of the last scenes we shot was the end of the film, where Angela is led away by the police. Our director, Mark, was way up high on an enormous camera crane and there were dozens of extras and police cars. As I stood waiting for my cue behind the big double doors at the front of the house, I once again couldn't believe my great fortune: My romantic screen fantasies had turned into reality.

Immediately after shooting was complete I returned to New York while postproduction continued in L.A. I was experiencing such terrible withdrawal. I had never been so emotionally, intellectually, and creatively engaged. I would lie on my sofa and go over in my head, scene by scene, the entire movie as we shot it, imagining what it would look like on the screen. I didn't actually get to see the movie until many months later when it premiered at the Sundance Film Festival in Utah. As I sat with hundreds of people in the festival's largest screening room, I was suddenly struck by something: It amazed me that while I'd written the play, acted the play, written the screenplay and starred in the film, it still hadn't occurred to me how autobiographical the story was until I saw it on the screen. How could Aeschylus' *House of Atreus*, rewritten as a 1960s suspense movie, be so personal? I realized that afternoon that if you took all of the melodramatic plot twists away, *Die, Mommie, Die!* was, essentially, the story of an aunt who wants the love of her late sister's children, and of her great need to protect them. Tears flooded my eyes, and I was very embarrassed. I didn't want people to think that I was weeping over my own performance. I believe that all creative work ends up a self-portrait, whether the artist is aware of it or not. As the detritus of our lives comprises our dreams, so it is with creative writing. It made me see that the female roles that I've created for myself all of these years were more than satiric jabs at Hollywood legends. I first saw those movies as a child when I was living with a fragile, though indomitable, woman, and I think my aunt's image, perhaps even more than those of great actresses long gone, has inspired my work.

A few months later we screened *Die! Mommie! Die!* at the San Francisco Gay and Lesbian Film Festival. It was shown at the magnificent old movie palace, the Castro Theatre. As soon as the movie ended, a spotlight hit me at the back of the theatre, and I strode down the long aisle in a gold-sequined pant suit and red wig, very much like Susan Hayward in *Valley of the Dolls*. Please don't think me too full of myself, but the entire audience leapt to their feet. They really did. By the time I reached the stage I was quite overcome. The head of the festival, Michael Lumpkin, handed me a microphone and I just had to share with the audience how, when I was a child, I had seen Bette Davis speak after a screening of *Hush . . . Hush, Sweet Charlotte*, and now here I was doing the same. I truly had come full circle.

– New York City, 2008

Psycho Beach Party

FADE IN:

EXT. SMALL TOWN PIZZA PARLOR IN 1962 – B/W – NIGHT

In BLACK and WHITE, we see the pizza parlor – windows lit up, filled with people. The ROAR of a motorcycle is heard approaching.

A young drifter, EDDIE (22), pulls up on his motorcycle. He's seen Brando in *The Wild One* a few too many times.

INT. THE PIZZA PARLOR – NIGHT

Eddie bangs open the front door. The entire room trembles at the sight of Eddie's black leather jacket, tight jeans, greased hair, and curled lip.

VINCE, the friendly Italian owner, gingerly approaches him.

> VINCE
> Eddie, my friend, what can I do for you?

> EDDIE
> I want to talk to Diane.

> VINCE
> But she don't want to talk to you.

Eddie pushes past him, making his way to the cashier.

> VINCE (CONT'D)
> Please, don't make trouble.

Over the cashier's counter has been built a makeshift booth. It has a square slot revealing the cashier's face. The cashier is DIANE and her face is indeed worth revealing. She is gorgeous.

> EDDIE
> Diane, before you start squawking, lemme just tell ya that you're the most wonderful girl I've ever known.

> DIANE
> Nobody's been as sweet to me as you. You make me feel – make me feel beautiful.

But you are beautiful. Why do you always hide behind that booth? Lemme see all of you.

DIANE

Please, I'm begging you. Go away and don't ever come back.

EDDIE

Kiss me.

Vince, placing his hand on Eddie's shoulder, tries to intercede.

VINCE

Eddie, please, for the love of God, go away

EDDIE

Not until I get my kiss.

Violently, Eddie pulls down the fragile booth, exposing Diane in all of her horror. Diane has two extra heads sprouting out of her shoulders. One head is her zombified twin and the other looks rather like a middle-aged proctologist on a bender. Eddie recoils in revulsion.

DIANE

Please, don't look at me that way.

EDDIE

No! No! No!

CAMERA TRUCKS BACK and IN COLOR we see that the image we've been watching is a movie on a screen at a drive-in theater.

EXT. A DRIVE-IN, SOUTHERN CALIFORNIA, 1962 – NIGHT (COLOR)

A row of cars sits in front of a massive screen. In the center of the row, we settle on a 1961 Ford Fairlane.

INT. THE FORD FAIRLANE – NIGHT

Two teenagers, ANGIE and BOBBY, are furiously necking in the front seat. Bobby's busy unfastening her bra.

ANGIE

You're missing the whole movie.

BOBBY

Believe me I ain't missin' a thing.

A '59 FORD COUNTRY SQUIRE STATION WAGON

In the car closest to Angie and Bobby's, two teenage girls are seated in the front seats. One is FLORENCE, 16, a spunky tomboy. The other is her best friend BERDINE, 16, very intellectual and terminally nerdy.

> BERDINE
> No one understands Bettina. Her screen persona is a brilliant comment on the entire sociopolitical structure of stardom.

> FLORENCE
> (with pride)

Gee, Berdine, you get all that from *The Pizza Waitress with Three Heads*? Well, I guess we are the only ones watching the movie. These guys have only one thing on their minds.
> (innocently)
Want a wiener?

EXT. MAIN STREET – B/W NIGHT

In *The Pizza Waitress with Three Heads*, Diane has mutated into a fifty foot giant, flattening cars and crushing buildings in her wake. It's clear that these are cheaply made models. The police fire away at her. The giant waitress tries to deflect their bullets with her round tray.

EXT. THE CONCESSION STAND – NIGHT

Florence stands on line. In front of her is a statuesque and very voluptuous BEACH BABE. Florence looks down at her own flat chest and feels totally inadequate. She looks up and recognizes someone.

> FLORENCE
Hey, Lars!

LARS is a good-looking Swedish exchange student. With his blond flattop and dark-rimmed glasses, he could be anywhere from nineteen to twenty-six. He's holding a tray with two hot dogs, popcorn and Cokes.

> LARS
> (in a thick Swedish accent)
I love the smells of America; hotdogs, popcorn –

> FLORENCE
Car exhaust. Lars, being how you're from Sweden, the sex capital of the entire world, could you tell me what's wrong with me?

> LARS
Nothing's wrong with you.

FLORENCE

Suddenly every girl I know is boy crazy. Golly, if some dork stuck his tongue down my throat I'd barf. Yucch! I'd belt him. I'd kick him in the nuts.

LARS

You're just a typical American girl. One day soon you'll wake up and explode into a woman. Well, my date will be anxious for these buns to be hot. Bye-bye.

BOBBY'S FORD FAIRLANE

Bobby opens the car door and jumps out.

ANGIE

Where ya goin', lover?

BOBBY

Goin' to the head and get us a "you know what." Don't want my girl spending next Christmas in a home for unwed mamas.

Bobby closes the car door.

EXT. THE CONCESSION STAND — NIGHT

Florence sees RHONDA, a teenage girl in a wheelchair, rolling away from the counter with her tray of refreshments.

FLORENCE

Hey there, Rhonda.

RHONDA

Hello, Florence. Got yourself a heavy date? You're so attractive.

FLORENCE

I'm here with Berdine. You'd think it was a crime against the nation to go to a drive-in with more than kissy kissy stuff on your mind.

RHONDA

You do have a quaint way of looking at things. Is it true you're going to Europe at the end of the summer?

FLORENCE

No, we just have a Swedish exchange student staying with us.

RHONDA

I heard you were going to Denmark.

> FLORENCE

Where'd ya get that idea?

> RHONDA

I heard you were going there to have some sort of an operation.

> FLORENCE

An operation?

> RHONDA

Yeah, I heard you're having your dick cut off and turning into a girl.

> FLORENCE

That's not funny.

> RHONDA
> (wheeling away)

Kisses.

EXT. MAIN STREET – B/W NIGHT

Diane, the giant pizza waitress, lifts a car into the air and lets it crash at her feet.

IN ANOTHER CAR – A 1961 CHEVROLET IMPALA CONVERTIBLE

A blonde sex kitten, MARVEL ANN, 17, is seated in the backseat surrounded by five GUYS, all of whom are worshipping her like the teen Goddess that she is.

Marvel Ann is licking the edges of an ice cream sandwich. She notices a sexy dude in the next car. It is STARCAT (19), the perfect image of the clean-cut 1960's teen idol. He's got one arm around a GIRL. He has an ice cream sandwich in his other hand and he, too, is licking off the edges. Marvel Ann nudges BUDDY next to her.

> MARVEL ANN

Hey Pea-brain, who's that guy in the next car? You know him?

> BUDDY

Yeah, I know him.

> MARVEL ANN

Well?

> BUDDY

Calls himself Starcat. Dropped out of Northwestern and hangs out in Malibu with a bunch of surf bums. Strictly a loser from Loserville.

Marvel Ann catches Starcat's eye. Staring at each other, they both lick the edges off their ice cream sandwiches with more than nourishment on their minds.

INT. A PSYCHIATRIST'S OFFICE – B/W – DAY

Back in *The Pizza Waitress with Three Heads*, DR. WENTWORTH, a distinguished scientist with the obligatory moustache and goatee, explains the case to the police.

> WENTWORTH
> Sergeant, the young woman is a victim of nuclear testing. Her cells appear to be in a constant state of mutation, aggravated by intense sexual frustration.

EXT. THE CONCESSION STAND – NIGHT

Florence is next on line at the counter.

> COUNTERMAN
> Can I help you?

> FLORENCE
> Well, let's see. I'll have a frank and maybe with it – hmmm. Golly, I'm not sure. What would be good?

The counterman turns to the BEACH BABE next to her.

> COUNTERMAN
> (seductively)
> And what can I do for you, doll?

Florence is pissed off. She focuses on a display of paper cups decorated with a whimsical circular pattern.

Her eyes widen. She SLAMS her fist down on the counter. From her innermost depths, comes the voice of a completely different person; low, sexy, violent.

> FLORENCE
> Who do you have to fuck to get a hot dog in this dump?

The counterman and the girl do a big double-take.

> COUNTERMAN
> Say what?

FLORENCE
You heard me, Buster. And I'm not paying extra for dialogue so cut the chin music.

The stunned counterman hurries with her order.

EXT. MAIN STREET – B/W NIGHT

In *The Pizza Waitress with Three Heads*, the giant Diane continues on her rampage.

INTERCUT: THE DRIVE-IN – THE FORD FAIRLANE – NIGHT

As Angie waits for Bobby to return, a gloved hand reaches for the door of Angie's car.

Inside, Angie notices the door handle turning. She sits up, then realizes it isn't Bobby.

ANGIE
Hey –

Her look of calm recognition turns to one of sheer terror as the black-and-white movie image is reflected on the blade of a large knife.

EXT. MAIN STREET – B/W NIGHT

Diane is hit by a barrage of bullets and falls to the ground, knocking over a building in the process.

EXT. THE FORD FAIRLANE – NIGHT

Berdine notices something in a nearby car. She goes over to investigate. She looks inside and sees Angie's bloody corpse.

A tight close-up of Berdine's bespectacled face as she SCREAMS in horror as we –

ROLL CREDITS

A frenetic GO-GO GIRL does a wildly athletic shimmy under the title. The credits bounce over her boobs as they shake to a rock and roll theme song.

EXT. A SUBURBAN STREET – DAY

Berdine and Florence are walking down the street.

BERDINE
It was horrible. So much blood. Like something out of Dostoyevsky. What took you so long at the snack bar?

I was about to order and the next thing I knew the guy at the counter went AWOL for some sweater job.

They are about to cross the street when a police car screeches around the corner and pulls up less than a foot in front of them.

The car door opens and a pair of shapely legs emerges from the vehicle. They belong to CAPTAIN MONICA STARK, the glamorous but briskly efficient homicide detective with the L.A. Sheriff's department. The car's driver is DET. WANDA "COOKIE" MOLASKEY. Cookie is a tall, heavyset, and very butch woman in her thirties.

MONICA
Captain Monica Stark, L.A. Sheriff's Department.

COOKIE
Detective Molaskey.

MONICA
Now don't tell me. Florence, Berdine.

BERDINE
Wow. You're good.

MONICA
It's my job. I understand you both were at the drive-in last night.

FLORENCE
Yeah. Berdine's the gal who found the body.

MONICA
Girls, I'd like to know exactly what you heard and exactly what you saw.

BERDINE
It's hard because I was concentrating on the subtext of the film.

MONICA
What about you, Florence?

FLORENCE
I guess I was on my way back from the snack bar.

MONICA
Did you notice anything unusual? Anything at all?

To be honest, the whole night's something of a blur. I bet some rat fink spiked my orangeade. Ha, ha, ha.

A 1960 Chrysler Dodge Dart pulls up to the curb. The driver is Florence's mother, MRS. FORREST. Think Lana Turner in *Peyton Place*, blonde hair in a neat French twist, the world's loveliest mom but there's a raging flame hidden beneath the charming exterior.

MRS. FORREST
(warmly)

Hello, girls.

FLORENCE

Hi, Mom.

MRS. FORREST

Florence, hop in. I thought you were going to help me pickle those beets.

FLORENCE

I was just on my way.
(to Monica)
Got to skedaddle. Tootles.

MONICA

We haven't quite finished.

Looking concerned, Mrs. Forrest gets out of the car.

MRS. FORREST

May I ask what's going on here?

COOKIE

There was a murder at the drive-in last night. White female, 17, sleeping it off in the morgue.

MRS. FORREST

A murder?
(to Florence)
And you didn't tell me?

FLORENCE

I didn't want to upset you.

MONICA

What were you doing around nine p.m., Mrs. Forrest?

MRS. FORREST

What any woman should be doing at that hour. Needlepoint.

MONICA

Yes. Well, Florence, if you wouldn't mind answering a few more questions, I'd gladly –

MRS. FORREST
(interrupts)
I don't think so. We have beets to pickle and Florence has to practice her oboe. She has a recital coming up.

MONICA

But Mrs. Forrest –

MRS. FORREST

Florence, dear, the car.

Florence gets into the car.

COOKIE

Now just one minuto, Sister, before we toss you both into a holding tank.

Mrs. Forrest moves to the side of her car.

MRS. FORREST

Show me a subpoena, Flatfoot.
(to Monica)
Madame Detective, I will not have my daughter bullied by the Secret Police. As far as I know, we are not yet a part of the Soviet Union.

Mrs. Forrest climbs into the car and zooms off.

Monica watches the car go, very intrigued by this mother/daughter duo.

INT. THE FORREST KITCHEN – DAY

Florence and Mrs. Forrest enter the kitchen and find Lars, the Swedish exchange student, carrying a large duffel bag.

LARS

Good afternoon, Mrs. Forrest. Florence.

MRS. FORREST

Where are you off to with that enormous satchel? Robbing a bank?

                              LARS
Laundry time.

                          MRS. FORREST
Leave that to me, Lars. It's women's work.

                              LARS
Oh, I do not wish to impose myself on you.

                          MRS. FORREST
Nonsense. It would be a pleasure. I haven't washed a man's
personal things since Mr. Forrest passed on.

                              LARS
Perhaps it's time you considered remarriage.

                          MRS. FORREST
Lars, you're outrageous. I lost two husbands in the big war and
one in Korea. My future lies in my widow's pensions – I mean
pension. Now off with you. You'll find everything folded on your
bed.

                              LARS
Mrs. Forrest, as Florence would say, "you are fantabulous."

Lars exits out the door.

                          MRS. FORREST
Well, they know how to grow 'em in Sweden.

She turns on the faucet, digs into the laundry bag, and takes out a
jockstrap. She pours detergent on it.

                            FLORENCE
Mother, can't you throw that in the machine?

                          MRS. FORREST
Darling, you know I'm a perfectionist. Just look at these urine
stains. They may never come out completely.

With cheerful fervor, she scrubs the jock strap. Something about her
mother washing the jock strap disturbs Florence.

EXT. THE BEACH – DAY

A bright, sunny day. Rocks leading to the beach. The teenage
sexpot, Marvel Ann leads the charge, followed by Florence and
Berdine.

Marvel Ann, I can't believe you called. I honestly thought you'd written me off as the geekiest geek of all time.

MARVEL ANN

Keep moving.

FLORENCE

We've never been to Malibu. What made you want to come here?

MARVEL ANN

I have my reasons.

BERDINE

Wait a minute, guys. I feel my nose blistering. I gotta put some –

MARVEL ANN

If you dare put any of that disgusting white gook on your nose, I will wring your scrawny neck until your eyes bug out.

BERDINE

Sorry, but I happen to be allergic to the sun.

FLORENCE

It's true. Her face turns fire engine red, her lips blow up –

BERDINE

And I get this terrible chafing between my legs.

MARVEL ANN

Spare me the details, Berdine.

The girls spread out the large beach blanket.

FLORENCE

Darn, I left my goggles and flippers in the car.

Marvel Ann strips down to her bikini.

MARVEL ANN

Florence, I think you've forgotten the reason we're here. This is a man hunt. Let's set our traps.

All three girls simultaneously put on their dark sunglasses. They focus on a group of surfers riding the waves. Marvel Ann leads the girls in posing seductively to lure the boys.

FLORENCE

Why do we have to bother with them? Can't we have a good time by ourselves?

MARVEL ANN

Don't be a dip. You've got the sex drive of a Milk Dud. You're
sixteen. Girl, get with the action. Just look at that water,
overflowing with boys.

Florence looks toward the ocean.

HER POV

The group of surfers ride the waves like a roller-coaster.

Their grace and skill is exhilarating.

FLORENCE is completely entranced. She almost hyperventilates.

FLORENCE

Wow, those guys are flying over those waves. It's the rompin',
stompin', livin' end!

EXT. BEACH – DAY

The surfers carry their boards out of the water.

Marvel Ann recognizes Starcat, the boy she was eyeballing at the
drive-in.

MARVEL ANN

I'm heading down to the water. You guys stay here and wait for
my signal.

BERDINE

They look like beatniks. Should I unpack my bongos?

MARVEL ANN

I intend to unpack mine.

Marvel Ann pushes her breasts forward and heads for the water.

Meanwhile, the surfers lean their boards against a nearby fence. They
are indeed a group of young beatniks, rebellious drop-outs but not
scary at all. PROVOLONEY, 21, is a scrappy kid with a lot of big ideas.
YO YO, 21, is the male equivalent of the dumb blonde, bulging with
muscles and not very bright. T.J. is slightly older and girl crazy.
JUNIOR, 21, is a good-looking guy who keeps his body covered up
with a large football jersey.

YO YO

Flip my fins, Daddy-O, see me getting tubed on that outsider?

PROVOLONEY
I got a tube for you. Why don't you ride this.

Provoloney gets Yo Yo's head in a vise grip. A wrestling match breaks out. Marvel Ann has moved close to the group but the guys, immersed in their frat boy roughhousing, don't even see her. Marvel Ann strikes goddess-like poses, letting the wind blow her hair away from her face.

The guys continue to cheer Yo Yo and Provoloney on as Provoloney attempts to pull Yo Yo's bathing suit off.

Marvel Ann looks increasingly irritable as she pushes her breasts forward, straining to compete with the exhibition of male bonding. She has one more weapon left. Marvel Ann loosens the straps of her bikini top. She screams as it falls off, and she has to hold the bikini top on.

MARVEL ANN
Oh no. What am I going to do?

Starcat breaks away from the group to come to her aid.

MARVEL ANN (CONT'D)
This is so embarrassing. I could die. Could you help me tie my straps?

STARCAT
You know, this could be an unconscious reflex of an over stimulated libido.

MARVEL ANN
Say, that sounds dirty.

Starcat adjusts her bikini top.

STARCAT
Sorry. I'm a refugee from the Psych Department at Northwestern. Name's Starcat. You were at the drive-in last night, weren't you?

MARVEL ANN
Uh huh, I'm Marvel Ann. I'm surprised you remember me. There was a lot going on. I mean, that girl getting her throat slashed and all.

STARCAT
She wasn't the only one murdered. You killed me with that look.

Florence and Berdine have followed Marvel Ann to the water.

THE SCREENPLAYS OF CHARLES BUSCH

Those your friends?

MARVEL ANN

Hardly. The one with the Coke bottles on her eyes has something that resembles a car. My folks took my wheels away cuz I ran over some old lady in a crosswalk. Boy, parents are such squares.

Florence runs over to them with Berdine in tow.

FLORENCE

That was so nifty. You guys were racing over those waves like a comet. I've never seen anything like it.

STARCAT

Excuse me.

FLORENCE

I'm Florence. Gosh, how'd you learn to do that?

MARVEL ANN

Florence, would you mind – .

BERDINE

Maybe we should get some lunch.

The other surfers join them.

FLORENCE

You guys were boss. You make it look so darn easy.

T.J.

Easy? Takes years to fly on top of the soup.

STARCAT

You gotta learn how to stay in the curl. There's also turning, stalling, trimming, riding the nose.

PROVOLONEY

Duck dives. Gliding through a wipeout.

T.J.

Knowing your way around point breaks, reef breaks, shore breaks.

YO YO

Doing the turtle. Nose dips.

Switch stance. Spinners.

FLORENCE

Wow!

Marvel Ann, jealous, grabs hold of Starcat's arm.

MARVEL ANN

I just love to watch.

FLORENCE

I want to learn. Mind if I tag along with you guys the next time you go out?

The guys get a big laugh out of this.

STARCAT

Forget it. Girls can't surf. The male of the species are natural born hunters and our prey is the perfect wave. I mean, heck, a surf board's even a phallic symbol.

Yo Yo looks at his long, smooth surfboard in a new way.

FLORENCE

Well, I don't know about that phallic stuff but I'm a terrific swimmer and a quick study.

YO YO

The great Kanaka would cool to subzero if we let a chick tag along.

FLORENCE

Who's the great Kanaka?

T.J.

Only the greatest surfer of all time. The Pope.

FLORENCE

Well, maybe he'll teach me how to surf.

The guys bust a gut laughing at that one.

STARCAT

Kanaka's a world champion. He's not gonna splash around with a half-pint like you.

FLORENCE

Well, how about you? Are you too big a fish to teach a girl?

PROVOLONEY
Ooh, Starcat has a fan. Ain't he simply gorgeous? Hold me close, you great big hunk of he-man.

Provoloney tries to kiss Starcat who pushes him away.

STARCAT
Knock it off.
(to Florence)
Kid, listen to it in high fidelity stereophonic sound. Surfing's a man's domain. No minnows in the shark tank.

Marvel Ann wraps herself around Starcat.

MARVEL ANN
I guess the fella's not interested.

Marvel Ann moves toward the ocean.

MARVEL ANN (CONT'D)
Oh no. I'm afraid of sharks. All points bulletin for a big, strong hero.

Marvel Ann runs into the water and the guys follow, hooting and hollering.

EXT. NEENIE'S FAMOUS WEINIES – DAY

Florence and Berdine are seated at the open-air snack bar adjacent to the beach. They're eating foot long hotdogs.

FLORENCE
There is no reason in the world why I can't be one of them. I gotta ingratiate myself. But how?

BERDINE
Those guys are interested in only two things and you don't have either of them.

Florence adjusts her top and sees Junior, the surfer wearing the football jersey, carrying his tray to a table.

As Junior passes her by, Florence sticks out her foot and trips him. He lands flat on his back. His food is scattered everywhere. Florence helps him up.

JUNIOR
There went lunch and I was down to my last peso.

FLORENCE

Well, like hey, you can have the rest of my hotdog. And Berdine, you don't want that Coke.

Florence grabs the Coke and hands it to Junior.

BERDINE

Hey –

FLORENCE
(interrupts)

Sit down. Take a load off.

Junior sits with them. Florence looks at Berdine indicating "Pretty good, huh?" Junior dives into the hotdog.

JUNIOR

Thanks for the chow.

FLORENCE

How come you stay all covered up? Afraid of a little sunburn? It's good for you.

JUNIOR

I suffer from the heartbreak of psoriasis. My back is covered with the stuff.

FLORENCE

Oh, I'm sorry. But that um football jersey looks really neato. Tell me, um what's the great Kanaka really like? Is he nice? A lot of laughs?

Junior attempts to speak after wolfing down his food.

JUNIOR

Kanaka moves to a different bop. He's the tiptop kaleidoscope of the cool.

FLORENCE

Does he live around here? I can't even imagine where someone that fantabulous would call home except maybe the White House.

JUNIOR

Kanaka has a place at the far end of the beach. Hey, you wouldn't be thinking of crashing his pad?

EXT. KANAKA'S SHACK – DAY

Indeed, Florence has gone in search of the great Kanaka.

Florence comes across a small beach shack with a large and rather terrifying carved Tiki guarding the door.

She peeks into a window. No one seems to be home. She opens the door and steps inside.

INT. KANAKA'S SHACK – DAY

The cabin is filled with shrunken heads, native masks, and pin-up calendars. Florence picks up a kitsch figurine of a naked woman.

A dark, brooding face suddenly appears over her shoulder. Florence screams and drops the figurine. Before it lands on the floor, it's caught by the great KANAKA.

He's a good-looking guy in his early thirties. He would seem like an oracle of great worldly wisdom if you were sixteen and had never traveled east of the San Diego Freeway.

> KANAKA
> What are you doing snooping around my shack?

> FLORENCE
> Are you . . . the Great Kanaka?

> KANAKA
> I am the man who rides the waves from Jay-pan to the Yucatan.

> FLORENCE
> I'm Florence. Wow. This is like meeting Walt Disney or Helen Keller. You're a living legend.

> KANAKA
> Hey, pour some water on the carburetor.

She picks up a shrunken head off the table.

> FLORENCE
> Hey, is this thing real?

> KANAKA
> You break it. You buy it. Now, what brings you to Kanaka's shack?

FLORENCE

Oh please, Great Kanaka, I want to learn how to surf. None of
the other guys will teach me. I'm desperate.

KANAKA

Oh yeah, we'd make quite a pair. Sorry Kid, go back to Mama
and Papa Square.

Florence eyes a naked Balinese statue of Shiva.

FLORENCE

If I looked like this, I bet you'd teach me.

KANAKA

Pussycat, if you looked like that, we'd be doing more than
chewing the fat.

Florence's eyes focus on Kanaka's shirt with its pattern of concentric
circles. They begin to animate and change colors and swirl.

KANAKA (CONT'D)

Numero uno, the water's what I crave. More than anything, I live
for Mother Wave.

Florence is possessed by an alternate self, a voracious vixen with a
low, seductive growl. She climbs onto his bed and strikes a 1950s
Betty Page pin-up pose.

FLORENCE

More than anything, I live for Father Fuck.

KANAKA

Florence?

FLORENCE

I'm afraid you've got the wrong girl. Florence is not my name.

KANAKA

Who are you?

FLORENCE

My name is Ann Bowman.
                    (fingers his fly)
I'm revealing my true nature.

KANAKA

Look, Jailbait, if I didn't live by my personal code of honor, I'd
take advantage of this situation erotically, as it were.

FLORENCE

I thought you were the man with the big cigar. What are you packin', a Tiparillo?

KANAKA

More than you can handle, kid. Now before I get mad, kindly vacate my pad.

Kanaka goes to the door.

FLORENCE

Don't you turn your butt to me!!

KANAKA

Florence?

FLORENCE
(screaming)
I am not Florence! My name is Ann Bowman! Ann Bowman! Ann Bowman!!

She jumps off the bed and blocks the door with her body.

KANAKA

Yeah, that's right. Ann Bowman.

FLORENCE

I frighten you, don't I?

KANAKA

I ain't scared.

FLORENCE

You're lying. Look at your hands. They're shakin' like Jell-o.

KANAKA

No, they ain't.

FLORENCE

You're scared. Say it! You're scared!

KANAKA

Yes!

FLORENCE

Yes, what?

KANAKA

Yes, ma'am!

FLORENCE

Ah, that's better. You're just a little slave boy, aren't you, sonny?

KANAKA

Ma'am, if you would, I ain't feelin' so good.

FLORENCE

Listen, Slime, can the nursery rhyme. I know what you fantasize about. I know what you dream about and I'm going to give it to you in spades. To start, I think I'll walk you down to the beach on a leash. Capiche?

KANAKA

But what will the rest of the fellas think?

FLORENCE

To hell with the rest of the fellas! I am the most important! Me! Ann Bowman! I will not be cast aside, I will not be –

Florence suddenly turns back into herself again.

FLORENCE (CONT'D)

– told a girl can't surf. I mean, golly, today a girl can do all sorts of things, like being a – an executive secretary.

KANAKA

Ann?

FLORENCE

Ann? My name's Florence. Squaresville, but what the heck.

KANAKA

Do you remember what we were just talking about?

FLORENCE

Surfing lessons. Can we start tomorrow? I can see I'm wearing down your resistance.

KANAKA

Can say that again.

FLORENCE

Yippee! I gotta get moving. Gotta round up a surfboard, not so easy, and then tomorrow, we hit the old H2O. Tootles.

Florence skips out of Kanaka's shack, leaving him scratching his head in disbelief.

REAR SCREEN SEQUENCE

Cheesy rear-screen shots of Kanaka teaching Florence how to surf underscored by the Surfaris' "STORM SURF." The waves on the stock footage behind them are as big as skyscrapers.

Lesson one: she's crouched low at the front of his surfboard, Kanaka standing at the back, guiding them.

She's never known such ecstasy as this roller-coaster ride over the waves.

Lesson two: Florence is on her own board. Ignoring Kanaka's instructions, she tries to stand and capsizes the board.

Lesson three: Florence is standing, wobbly but standing on the board. Kanaka shouts instructions at her but they both end up falling on their asses.

EXT. THE BEACH – DAY

Kanaka and Florence carry their boards out of the water. The guys watch them, totally confused.

> FLORENCE
> I am sort of picking it up a little?

> KANAKA
> Yeah. Cool, baby, cool. You're a demon.

Florence steps on a sharp rock.

> FLORENCE
> (grunting)
> Ow!

> KANAKA
> Ann?

> FLORENCE
> Beg your pardon?

> KANAKA
> Nothing.

The guys join them.

> PROVOLONEY
> Kanaka, I don't mean to be scraping your fins but you can't let a

chick infiltrate our stag clan, man. That's how it starts. Next thing you'll be eating frozen waffles and wearing a cardigan.

> JUNIOR
> Yeah, you're the Emperor of the Seven Seas. This makes us all look cheap.

Kanaka, refusing to talk, examines his board for nicks.

> STARCAT
> Kanaka doesn't have to answer to anybody. If he wants to indulge this pipsqueaks' penis envy that's his business.

> FLORENCE
> Yeah. So there.

Florence realizes Starcat's line wasn't a compliment.

> T.J.
> Kanaka, I thought you had some hot babe you were seeing. You can't be that desperate.

> KANAKA
> Yeah well, that new chick's as complex as the zodiac. Never know when she's coming back.

Yo Yo spins Florence around.

> YO YO
> You're not even a chick. You're a "chicklet."

> FLORENCE
> Ha, ha, ha.

> PROVOLONEY
> Yeah, that should be your name. Don't you dig it? I hereby dub you "Chicklet."

> KANAKA
> It'll pass. The name's got class.

From here on Florence will be called Chicklet.

> CHICKLET
> I buy it. I buy it. I'll be Chicklet. Does this mean I'm part of the gang?

T.J. makes a wolf whistle. To the tune of the Pastel Six "STRANGE GHOST," a gorgeous woman (BETTINA) in a bathing suit, large movie star sunglasses and an enormous sun hat leaves her beachfront house. Climbing down the steps to the sand, she loses her courage, and runs back into the house.

> T.J.
> There's some prize tomatoes in that can.

> YO YO
> I didn't think anybody lived in the Elkins House.

> KANAKA
> For good reason.

> CHICKLET
> How come?

> PROVOLONEY
> Because it's haunted.

> CHICKLET
> Really? Have you ever been inside?

> T.J.
> In my time. There are ghosts all right. I could feel it in my nuts.

> STARCAT
> You and your nuts.

> T.J.
> I've had a man's hairy balls since I was eight. It's the source of my power. They tell me the weather, time of day, and if there's a pile-up on Route 66.

> CHICKLET
> Did something really awful happen in that house?

> JUNIOR
> Oh yeah. A bunch of people died there.

> KANAKA
> (brooding)
> Some people were born to die.

Kanaka stalks away. But then Kanaka's always a little weird.

INT. AUGIE'S COFFEE SHOP – DAY

A brand new Googie style coffee shop, slanted ceiling, toasters on the

tables. Berdine is seated in a booth by the window, waiting for
Chicklet.

The waitress, PAT, a long stringbean of a woman, is ready to take her
order.

>   PAT
> Berdine, hon, looks like your little friend is awfully late. Got a
> roastbeef au jus with your initials on it.

>   BERDINE
> No thanks. I'll wait a little longer.

The wheelchair-bound teenager, RHONDA, wheels by.

>   RHONDA
> Pat, I'm sorry you're going bald but finding clumps of hair in the
> chicken a la king frankly grossed me out. It's reflected in your
> gratuity.

>   PAT
> Why, I never . . . And my hair isn't –

>   RHONDA
> Hello, Berdine. You enjoy your own company, don't you?

>   BERDINE
> I'm waiting for Florence.

>   RHONDA
> You two used to be friends. Right?

>   BERDINE
> Florence is my best friend and she's gonna be here any minute.

EXT. THE BEACH – DAY

It's late afternoon. Starcat and Junior are holding Chicklet's arms,
while Yo Yo rubs his head against her stomach, giving her the Chinese
Tickle Torture. She's having the time of her life being one of the guys.
Two gorgeous girls stroll by. The boys drop Chicklet to the ground.

>   T.J.
> Ooh. Twin dips. Let's invite them to the luau.

>   KANAKA
> They'll do fine. T.J., toss 'em a line.

>   CHICKLET
> What luau?

PROVOLONEY

It's just the whippin', rippin', flippin', biggest event of the whole summer.

YO YO

A wild night. Know how to spell "orgy"?

CHICKLET

Better than you. I want to go.

STARCAT

Kid, you're definitely not the luau type.

T.J.

But those two angels are.

Everyone but Chicklet and Junior follows the two girls.

KANAKA

Junior, you coming?

JUNIOR

Nah. I'm sticking around. There's still some good shore breaks.

They shrug and move on. Junior picks up his board and heads for the water. Chicklet, feeling sexless and ignored, watches Junior's behind as he walks toward the water. On his ass are two perfect circles of sand from where his butt rested on the beach. Chicklet instantly turns into the seething Ann Bowman. She looks in the direction of the guys inviting the two girls to the luau. She growls to herself.

CHICKLET
(as Ann)

No man rejects Ann Bowman. Ann Bowman invented luaus. Ann Bowman invented orgies! Ann Bowman invented revenge!!

The sky dramatically darkens, reflecting Chicklet's personality change.

EXT. THE BEACH – DAY

The following day, all is sunny again. Chicklet, Starcat, T.J., Yo Yo, and Provoloney are arriving at the beach.

PROVOLONEY

Guys, any of you know a sure-fire cure for constipation? I got it real bad. It's wreckin my center of gravity.

STARCAT

It could be psychological. A secret or repressed longing can lead to anal retention.

CHICKLET

That's silly. My mom swears by enemas filled with beef broth and Epsom salts.

STARCAT

Bud out. Provoloney, we've got to dig deep, deep into that dark inner place where your fear lies.

PROVOLONEY

I'll take an Ex-Lax.

Kanaka, arriving at the beach from the opposite direction, joins them. All of his chest hair has been shaved off.

T.J.

On this fine morning, how is your Flipness?

KANAKA

His Flipness is ready to lead his troupe into the soup. Hey, where's Junior?

PROVOLONEY

Haven't seen him since yesterday.

STARCAT

Wasn't he with you, Chicklet?

CHICKLET

He was, I guess, for awhile.

YO YO

Kanaka, did you shave off all of your chest hair?

KANAKA
(embarrassed)

Well, you know, Olympic swimmers shave their body hair so's they can move faster through the water.

CHICKLET

Does your new lady friend like it that way?

KANAKA

Oh yeah, baby. My shave got a rave.

Provoloney sneaks around Yo Yo and yanks his bathing suit up between his butt cheeks.

PROVOLONEY

Wedgie attack!

Yo Yo tackles Provoloney. Soon a cheering CROWD of surfers have gathered to watch Yo Yo and Provoloney wrestle on the sand. T.J. squirts a bottle of tanning lotion over them. The effect of their bodies slathered in hot oil changes the tone of the horseplay. The line between macho rough-housing and erotic foreplay has been crossed. The surfers watching them look decidedly uncomfortable.

> STARCAT
> Hey guys, c'mon. That's enough.

Yo Yo grabs on to what he thinks is Provoloney's arm.

> YO YO
> Man, I've got you now!

Yo Yo pulls on the arm and a severed limb emerges from the sand. He holds it in horror.

> YO YO (CONT'D)
> What the hell is this?

Chicklet SCREAMS. Yo Yo drops the arm in revulsion.

> PROVOLONEY
> The bicep! It's got psoriasis on it.

> STARCAT
> Junior!

EXT. BEACH – DAY

Junior's body has been dug out of the sand and lies covered up with a sheet. The corpse is surrounded by friends, gawkers, and police.

Captain Monica Stark, struggling to maneuver through the sand in her high heels, approaches Cookie.

> MONICA
> How long was he planted there?

> COOKIE
> Maybe six hours. We've just located the pancreas, intestines, and right toe.

> MONICA
> And this group of deadbeats?

> COOKIE
> Alibis as tight as Sandra Dee's butt.

(points to Chicklet)

Except that one.

TIME CUT A FEW MINUTES LATER

Monica approaches Chicklet, who is standing near Kanaka.

MONICA

Well, here we are at yet another murder. I'd rather we met for miniature golf.

CHICKLET

He was my friend.

MONICA

I understand that at the time of the murder, you were walking along the beach. Run into anyone on this relaxing stroll?

Kanaka pushes in front of Chicklet, inventing a story.

KANAKA

I saw her. Chicklet, how come you didn't tell her I bought you a burger and fries?

MONICA

The great Kanaka. Leader of the pack.

KANAKA

Long time no see.

MONICA

Still following the sun?

KANAKA

Still walking the straight and narrow-minded?

MONICA

Still intend to knock down that firetrap you call a bachelor pad?

KANAKA

Come over with those handcuffs and we'll burn it down – together.

Monica knees him in the groin. He doubles over in pain.

MONICA

You forget that I'm both a cop and a lady.

PROVOLONEY

We didn't do nothing wrong. Why are you picking on us?

MONICA

Because I don't like you. Don't like the way you talk, don't like the way you walk. Don't like your haircut. You kids think you own this beach. Think it's a teenage world. Well, you're dead wrong.

CHICKLET

Are you gonna arrest us?

MONICA

I might. I've got methods that can get the truth out of the most hardened criminal. I have a special room. Picture if you will, cold steel, blinding lights. Formica coffee table.

YO YO

Ugh. I've heard enough.

MONICA

Well, you'll be hearing more from me. Especially you, Mr. Kanaka. Cookie?

She nods to Cookie and the two policewomen stalk away from the crime scene.

STARCAT

Kanaka, why's she got it in for you?

KANAKA

I boffed her once in West Covina.

Yo Yo and Chicklet walk together.

YO YO

Carving up Junior like a Thanksgiving turkey. How does a monster like that sleep at night?

CHICKLET
(very troubled)
If you're insane, you might not even remember you did it. You might not remember anything.

She breaks away and walks up the beach, wondering what in the world she did last night.

INT. THE LAUNDRY ROOM – NIGHT

Chicklet, unable to sleep, hears something and goes down into the laundry room. She finds Lars wearing only his pajama bottoms doing a wash.

> CHICKLET

Lars, it's two in the morning and you're doing laundry?

> LARS

Did I make too much noise?

> CHICKLET

Only to someone with insomnia.

> LARS

Why should you have trouble sleeping?

> CHICKLET

Inner demons.

> LARS

You ate too much of your mother's Beef Tournedos. If I didn't stop you, you would have taken all my meat.

> CHICKLET

Lars, haven't you heard? One of my friends was found murdered today. Hacked up to bits. And I was the last one to see him alive.

> LARS

Do you have any idea who would do such a terrible thing?

> CHICKLET

No, but then I wonder if maybe I did see something. But I can't remember. Like a mental block.

> LARS

It's very sad about your friend. You must not torture yourself. You are alive. You must go out and surf the waves. Just like your friend would have done. As my old grandmother Ingrid used to say, "Lars, *getoffen lueffen flueffen.*"

> CHICKLET

That's what she said, huh? I guess that does make me feel a little better.

Chicklet shrugs and returns to her room.

EXT. DOWN THE BEACH – DAY

Down the beach, the beautiful mystery woman the kids glimpsed earlier is lounging on a chaise on the beach directly in front of her deck. She is none other than the movie star, BETTINA BARNES, AKA "The Pizza Waitress with Three Heads."

Chicklet, YoYo, Provoloney, and T.J. jog by, quickly notice her and move in for an introduction.

> T.J.
> And then the Papa Bear said "Who's been sleeping in my sandbox?"

> BETTINA
> (with innocent breathiness)
> Am I trespassing? I had no idea.

> YO YO
> Say, you look real familiar.

> BETTINA
> No, I don't!

> T.J.
> Give us a clue. What's your name?

> BETTINA
> I'm afraid I can't answer that.

> CHICKLET
> Are you incognito?

> BETTINA
> No, I'm German-Irish.

Provoloney stares at Bettina who is seated with Chicklet and Yo Yo on either side of her.

> PROVOLONEY
> Wait a second. Chicklet, could you move a little to the left. A little more.

Chicklet moves closer to Bettina.

> PROVOLONEY (CONT'D)
> And Yo Yo, lean your head in closer. Keep going. Yeah, that's it.

Yo Yo moves his head close to Bettina's. She looks as though Chicklet and Yo Yo's heads are sprouting from her shoulders.

> PROVOLONEY (CONT'D)
> The Pizza Waitress with three heads!

> CHICKLET
> Bettina Barnes!

BETTINA

Shhhh. No one must know my true identity. You see, I ran away from the studio. You can't imagine what it's like being exploited by those lousy flesh peddlers and power brokers. Everyone wanting a little piece. I'm not a pepperoni.

T.J.

I caught you in that flick *Sex Kittens Go to Outer Space*.

BETTINA

That was a good film but then I had to do the four sequels. Quel trash. They have no respect for the rights of the individual.

YO YO

We'll respect you.

BETTINA

Would you really? I'm hiding out here until the studio agrees to my terms. Full script, director, and hairdo approval.

Berdine arrives on the scene.

BERDINE

Florence! There you are. Yesterday, I waited for you at Augie's for over two hours.

CHICKLET

Please, my name's "Chicklet."

BERDINE

Yes, you're definitely not Florence anymore.

Suddenly, Berdine recognizes Bettina and SCREAMS.

BERDINE (CONT'D)

Bettina Barnes!

The guys grab her and cover her mouth.

CHICKLET

She's in hiding.

BERDINE

Bettina Barnes. In person. I loved you in *The Tarantula Queen of Hoboken*. I swear I saw *Sex Kittens and the Killer Meatball* sixteen times.

BETTINA
(thrilled)
Did you really?

BERDINE
Oh yes, Miss Barnes. You are more than a mere sex kitten. You
are the feminine embodiment of the Nietzchian superman. Ever
striving, striking a blow for the truth in the eternal battle of the
sexes.

BETTINA
That's what I've been telling my agents for months. What's your
name?

BERDINE
Berdine. Always was Berdine. Always will be.

BETTINA
I desperately need a secretary slash companion slash masseuse.
How'd you like to have a job for the summer?

BERDINE
I'm really honored but Florence and I have a zillion things planned
and –

She sees Chicklet being tickled by Yo Yo and Provoloney and dissolved
in giggles.

BERDINE (CONT'D)
(with a new resolve)
I'd love to be your gal Friday. When do I start?

BETTINA
Pronto. Come inside. I'm going to let you into my private world.
We're gonna have a blast!

Bettina drags Berdine up the stairs to her deck.

EXT. THE BEACH – DAY

Chicklet carries her surfboard into the water.

REAR SCREEN SEQUENCE

Under Gene and the Esquires' "SPACE RACE," we see Chicklet
standing up on the surfboard trying to improve her style.

ON THE BEACH

Starcat walks along and sees her out in the water. He stops and watches her surf.

REAR SCREEN/IN THE WATER

For the first time Chicklet rides her surfboard with a smooth grace. Suddenly she's hit by a large wave, causing her board to fly up into the air. Chicklet is overtaken by the intense rush of whitewater.

ON THE BEACH

Starcat's concerned when she doesn't quickly appear in the water. He sees her board wash up but no Chicklet. He runs into the surf.

IN THE WATER

Starcat discovers Chicklet semi-conscious. He carries her back to the shore.

ON THE BEACH

He lies her down and tenderly holds her in his arms as she coughs up the seawater.

> STARCAT
> Are you okay?

Chicklet becomes aware of the intimate physical closeness between them. She's surprised at how much she likes it.

> CHICKLET
> How come you helped me? I thought you would have let me drown.

> STARCAT
> What would you say a crazy thing like that for?

> CHICKLET
> It's common knowledge that you hate me.

> STARCAT
> I don't hate you. I don't hate you at all. When you didn't come up, I suddenly thought – I thought –

Starcat begins to feel awkward having Chicklet in his arms.

> STARCAT (CONT'D)
> Doesn't she know she should dive before the wipeout?

CHICKLET

Of course I know that. It was an accident, but then you never have accidents, Mister Perfect.

Chicklet stands up and wipes off the sand.

STARCAT

Don't you ever call me that.

CHICKLET

What? Mister Perfect?

STARCAT

You don't know what it's like having everybody think you're the golden boy. Perfectly smart, perfectly athletic. You can't imagine the pressure.

CHICKLET

And I thought all those people starving in India had it bad.

STARCAT

It's a curse. But you're so wrapped up in trying to prove you're one of the guys, you've never given a thought to my personal anguish. Well, you're not a guy and you never will be. Why – why can't you be a normal girl like Marvel Ann?

CHICKLET

Oh, I wish I could be like her, so cultured, so refined. I can imagine all those wonderful evenings you've spent together at the opera, museums, reading the great books.

STARCAT

Aw, forget it. The next time you're drowning, you can save yourself.

Starcat walks away from her. Chicklet shouts at his departing figure.

CHICKLET

No matter how hard you try, you will always be perfect! Perfect! Perfect! Perfect! Perfect hair! Perfect teeth! Perfect Eyes!
                    (wistfully, to herself)
Perfectly perfect.

INT. BETTINA'S LIVING ROOM – DAY

Bettina is hooked up to a "fanny belt." The exercise machine's purpose is to firm up Bettina's already perfect butt. At the same time, she is attempting to read a script.

Berdine enters carrying a small framed photograph.

> BERDINE
> Miss Barnes. Miss Barnes?

Bettina shuts off the machine and throws the script against the wall.

> BETTINA
> Another lousy sci-fi horror flick. Berdine, I just can't identify with the Rat-faced Girl from Mars.

> BERDINE
> Is it really that bad?

> BETTINA
> (surprisingly tough)
> Honey, Lassie could fart out a better script.

> BERDINE
> Miss B, I found this photograph stuck away in a corner. Is this your family?

> BETTINA
> No, I've never seen it before.

There's a knock on the sliding glass doors. It's Chicklet, Starcat, Yo Yo, Provoloney, and T.J.

> BETTINA (CONT'D)
> Oh, come in. Come in.

The kids open the doors and enter.

> T.J.
> We brought you some flowers, but I guess my body heat sorta slaughtered 'em.

He takes the pathetic, wilted bouquet from behind his back.

> BETTINA
> You've got one hot body. Thanks.

> CHICKLET
> Hey there, Berdine. How's it – ?

Berdine takes the flowers from Bettina and leaves the room. Chicklet gets the point.

       THE SCREENPLAYS OF CHARLES BUSCH

BETTINA

Berdine just found this photo. Who could it be?

PROVOLONEY

Whoa. This here's the flip side of cool.

STARCAT

The Elkins Family.

CHICKLET

Are those the people who – ?

Starcat gives Chicklet a fierce look to clam up.

BETTINA

You can tell me. I like feeling tingles.

T.J.

Yeah, well baby, this tale even makes my massive cojones rise. Fifteen years ago, the Elkins family made this joint their digs. Ten year old Larry was the youngest of the three kids.

YO YO

One hot summer night, he couldn't sleep so he took his mama's sharpest carving knife and hacked 'em all to death.

BETTINA

Look at my goosebumps.

Berdine comes back into the room.

T.J.

They say the house is haunted. If you're scared, I'd like to make a pitch for being your bodyguard, all night long if need be.

BETTINA

Tres gallante.

BERDINE

Miss B, I've got an even better idea. I've a book at home on Balinese exorcism rituals. I bet I could get rid of those ghosts.

BETTINA

Quel fun! Let's do it.

T.J.
(disappointed)

Yeah, let's do it.

BETTINA
We'll have a slumber party chez moi and take a whack at some of those spells. That'll show those evil spirits who's boss.

INT. THE FORREST KITCHEN – DAY

Mrs. Forrest is hard at work on a very complicated dessert. Chicklet is her assistant chef.

MRS. FORREST
A slumber party thrown by a movie actress? Perhaps if it were Deborah Kerr or Audrey Hepburn, but Bettina Barnes? Out of the question.

CHICKLET
But Mom, it's not like we're going drag racing in Griffith Park.

MRS. FORREST
You're going to flip for this Bavarian custard pudding. Florence, please get the eggs out of the Frigidaire.

CHICKLET
But Mother –

MRS. FORREST
A slumber party is an invitation to sexual intercourse. Oh, I know how they paint it in the movies. A man and a woman locked in embrace, soft lighting, a pitcher of Manhattans, Rachmaninoff in the background. Well, my girl, that is not how it is. You don't know how repugnant it can be having a man's sweaty thing poking at you.

FLORENCE
Mother!

MRS. FORREST
How does that feel? You like that?

Mrs. Forrest jabs Chicklet in the arm with her finger.

CHICKLET
Stop. You're hurting me.

MRS. FORREST
That's nothing compared to when they poke you down there!

Chicklet looks at her mother's polka dot apron and instantly turns into a very tough, street-wise young black woman named Tylene.

CHICKLET
(as Tylene)
Get them ugly old paws off me, Bitch!

MRS. FORREST
Florence!

CHICKLET
(as Tylene)
Don't you tell me how to handle a man's flippety-floppety. Baby, I grease up the cake pan, throw it in the oven, and let the batter rise.

MRS. FORREST
Florence, stop it!

Chicklet slaps her mother across the face. Mrs. Forrest recoils and starts to cry. Chicklet snaps out of it.

CHICKLET
Mother, what's wrong? Why are you crying?

MRS. FORREST
(at a loss)
You never know, do you? I must be the worst mother in the entire world.

CHICKLET
No, it's just that things are different from when you were young. But it doesn't mean they're bad.

MRS. FORREST
You really want to go to that party, don't you?

CHICKLET
It's the non-stop ultimate. I'll die if I miss it.

MRS. FORREST
Well, as long as there will be no boys present, I suppose it's as you teens would say "Okle dokle."

INT. BETTINA'S LIVING ROOM – NIGHT

Candles are lit, incense burning. We PAN across the decidedly male faces of Yo Yo, Provoloney, and T.J., coming to rest on Starcat. As Marvel Ann snuggles up next to him, Chicklet stares at her with a new kind of jealousy. Indeed, the entire room is a powder keg of frustrated passion. Even Yo Yo and Provoloney exchange furtive glances.

Berdine, wearing a home-made Balinese headdress composed of plastic forks, sits next to Bettina, who's in the throes of spiritual ecstasy.

> BETTINA
>
> I feel the spirit's hot breath on my neck. A touch, fingers lightly caressing my breast. Their lips on mine. So sweet. A tongue, a tongue licking my-

> BERDINE
>
> Good gravy, I forgot the chant! That's supposed to come first.

Bettina is jarred out of her erotic reverie. The guys are ready to murder Berdine.

> T.J.
>
> We were doing just swell.

> BETTINA
>
> Why don't we take a break and I'll whip up the specialite de maison, my world famous jalapeno pancakes with peach sauce?

INT. BETTINA'S KITCHEN – NIGHT

Bettina is whisking the pancake batter and covered with it. T.J. is leaning over her. In contrast to Mrs. Forrest's immaculate kitchen, this one is a culinary disaster area.

> BETTINA
>
> Look at me. I'm hopeless.

> T.J.
>
> I'll get that.

He leans down and tries to lick the batter off her cleavage. Bettina pushes him away.

> BETTINA
>
> Stop. I think it's best if we preserve the fantasy of my screen image.

Bettina starts to leave, then turns back and whispers to T.J. . . . .

> BETTINA (CONT'D)
> Meet me in the guest bathroom in ten minutes.

Bettina slithers out of the kitchen, leaving T.J. breathless.

INT. THE UPSTAIRS HALLWAY – NIGHT

Provoloney and Yo Yo snoop around. Provoloney opens a door. It's Bettina's boudoir.

THE SCREENPLAYS OF CHARLES BUSCH

INT. BETTINA'S BEDROOM — NIGHT

The room is decorated in the height of movie star excess; round bed, mirrors galore.

                    PROVOLONEY
        Dig this. Must be Bettina's room.

Provoloney opens the doors to an armoire and it overflows with feather boas and filmy peignoirs. The two boys look like they've just opened the door to Munchkinland.

INT. BETTINA'S LIVING ROOM — NIGHT

Alone in the living room, Chicklet studies the photo of the Elkins family. Starcat enters. His presence startles Chicklet.

                    STARCAT
        It's just me, Starcat.

                    CHICKLET
        Sorry. I'm sure Larry Elkins is residing in a well-guarded booby
        hatch somewhere.

                    STARCAT
        Unless the State Board of Evaluation found his treatment and
        rehabilitation to be complete. Then he could get sprung.

                    CHICKLET
        As an expert on human psychology, maybe you can help me. I
        have this girlfriend. I'm kind of worried about her. She has these
        . . . blackouts.

                    STARCAT
        What sort of blackouts?

                    CHICKLET
        Well, she says that when she comes to, she can't remember
        anything that happened but she has this funny feeling that when
        she's out, she's like really out. I mean, like out of her bird. Well,
        what do you think?

                    STARCAT
        It's not professional to give an instant diagnosis, but I'd say she's
        definitely suffering from morbidly psychotic episodes of
        schizophrenia. I didn't know Berdine was so unstable.

                    CHICKLET
        Berdine? Who said anything about Berdine?

STARCAT
Well, you don't have any other friends.

CHICKLET
(getting steamed)
Twisted loner that I am?

STARCAT
I'm sorry. I didn't mean it like that. How's about a truce?

CHICKLET
Okay, a truce and I take it back that you're perfect. You're deeply
flawed. In fact, from a certain angle, I can even see a small bump
on your nose.

STARCAT
From one mess to another?

Starcat extends his arms and they hug. Chicklet feels an incredible
sexual tingle. She's facing a large portrait of Bettina done in the style
of the sixties artist Keene. The portrait's eyes are enormous – the
pupils large dark circles. They begin to animate and spin and change
colors.

STARCAT (CONT'D)
I guess the reason I pick on you is cause you're so darn perky. You
can't help it. Not all of us can be attuned to the dark side of life.

Marvel Ann appears at the door. She sees Chicklet's face over Starcat's
shoulder. Unbeknownst to Starcat, Chicklet has turned into Ann
Bowman. She looks at Marvel Ann with an evil leer and silently
mouths "Fuck you."

MARVEL ANN
Starcat, I'm here. Remember me, Marvel Ann?

Marvel Ann grabs Starcat's arm and leads him away.

INT. UPSTAIRS BATHROOM – NIGHT

T.J. looks around the bathroom, entranced by all the sexy pin-up
photos of Bettina decorating every surface of the room. He spots her
framed *Playboy* centerfold and begins to stroke it tenderly. There's a
knock on the door.

T.J.
Mmm, is that the lady of my dreams?

T.J. unlocks the door. What he sees renders him speechless.

Wha . . .

An unseen figure comes toward T.J. with an upraised knife and plunges it into his chest.

INT. BETTINA'S BEDROOM – NIGHT

Yo and Provoloney are looking through her closet. Yo Yo is wearing a large hat covered with white ostrich feathers.

YO YO
Imagine Bettina wearing this stuff.

PROVOLONEY
Yeah, and naked underneath.

Provoloney lifts a chiffon negligee off its hanger.

PROVOLONEY (CONT'D)
Can't you just see her pretty titties bouncing under this one?

YO YO
Let me see. Which is the top?

Yo Yo puts it on and is enveloped in white ostrich feathers.

YO YO (CONT'D)
Try this on. It looks your size.

He hands a filmy bedjacket to Provoloney who tries it on.

PROVOLONEY
I don't know. Kinda makes my neck look thick.

Just then, Bettina opens the door. The two boys are frozen in shock.

PROVOLONEY (CONT'D)
We . . . we were just looking around for stuff for the exorcism.

YO YO
We didn't hurt anything. Honest.

BETTINA
Of course you didn't. Those white feathers look great against your tan.
(to Provoloney)
But I don't think beige is your color at all. Put on my black peignoir. It's a Paris original.

Oh, I – uh – I . . .

BETTINA

There's nothing wrong with dressing up. That's why I'm an actress. Some afternoon, you should come over and we can play beauty parlor.

Provoloney and Yo Yo quickly throw off their "drag."

PROVOLONEY

Sure. We better get downstairs. The guys will be looking for us.

YO YO

Yeah, yeah. The guys.

The two boys scoot out of the room like bats out of Hell.

BETTINA

But you haven't even seen my shoes.

INT. BETTINA'S FOYER – NIGHT

Chicklet and Berdine are looking at themselves in a mirror, each applying one of Bettina's many lipsticks that they've found in a bowl.

CHICKLET

Berdine, have I been acting strange lately?

BERDINE

Other than being an obnoxious snob?

CHICKLET

That bad, huh?

BERDINE

It's okay. You're part of the cool crowd now. Being best friends and soul-mates is sort of kids' stuff. As Jean Paul Sartre would say –

CHICKLET

What I meant was, do you think I'm suffering from morbidly psychotic episodes of schizophrenia?

BERDINE

Morbidly schizophrenic what? Where'd you get that crazy idea?

CHICKLET

It's like just now, I was talking to Starcat, and the next thing I know I'm out here with you.

                            BERDINE
Does this happen a lot?

                            CHICKLET
Well, the last time it happened was the night Junior was killed.

Suddenly a monstrous face appears in the mirror behind them. The girls SCREAM and spin around. The monster is Kanaka with a flashlight under his chin.

                        CHICKLET (CONT'D)
Kanaka, you ratfink!

                            KANAKA
                          (laughing)
Don't give me no sass. It was a gas.

A truly bloodcurdling, trademark Bettina Barnes SCREAM is heard from upstairs.

Kanaka and the girls race upstairs.

INT. UPSTAIRS BATHROOM – NIGHT

Chicklet, Berdine, and Kanaka join Starcat, Marvel Ann, Yo Yo, and Provoloney. They see T.J. lying nude in the tub with a knife plunged in his chest. Bettina sobs hysterically.

                            STARCAT
Nobody touch anything.

TIME CUT

INT. UPSTAIRS BATHROOM – NIGHT

Captain Monica and Cookie examine T.J.'s corpse.

                            MONICA
Cookie, is there something stuffed in his mouth?
                        (She looks closer)
Oh my God.

INT. BETTINA'S LIVING ROOM – NIGHT

Several cops are questioning each of the members of the party in different parts of the house. Monica passes by each of them, catching snippets of their overlapping dialogue. She walks by Yo Yo and Provoloney.

> PROVOLONEY
> . . . Somebody's bumping off all of our friends. I don't wanna die!
> I'm panicking! I tell ya, it's giving me . . .

Monica catches some of Starcat.

> STARCAT
> . . . severe feelings of loss and a profound sense of anxiety.

Marvel Ann's shrill voice reaches Monica's ears.

> MARVEL ANN
> I suppose this is your answer to school over-crowding, letting us
> get butchered one by one?

Monica passes by Chicklet and Berdine, who are being questioned by
Cookie.

> CHICKLET
> We were trying on lipsticks when we heard Bettina.

> BERDINE
> I'd know that scream anywhere – tender and vulnerable . . . yet
> brimming with inner strength.

Monica finds Bettina huddled on the sofa, sobbing.

> MONICA
> Miss Barnes, I hope my colleagues weren't too rough on you.

> BETTINA
> No, I'll be all right. This trauma can only make me a greater
> artist . . .

While Bettina continues talking, Monica sees Kanaka being questioned
across the room. Bettina's voice trails off as Monica becomes lost in a
memory of ten years earlier.

FLASHBACK

INT. SQUAD CAR – 1952 – NIGHT

In a parked squad car in a dark alley, a man and a woman are making
passionate love. They're nude except for their police caps. The woman
is Monica and the man is Kanaka! She sits on top of him in the front
seat.

> MONICA
> Keep it going, Pardner. Pick up the speed.

Tight close-up of him kissing her breast. It's very obvious that Monica's nude form is that of a body double.

Close-up of Monica's face.

> MONICA (CONT'D)
> Harder. Shift gears. Pull back. Now run the light.

The moonlight illuminates the soft curve of her hips and arched back . . . Kanaka sits up.

> MONICA (CONT'D)
> What's wrong?

> KANAKA
> Taking a breather. I spoke with Sergeant MacIlhenny. He said we could have the wedding in his backyard. And Steve Casey's wife said she'd do the flowers.

> MONICA
> You've been busy.

> KANAKA
> If we want a June wedding.

> MONICA
> Isn't that a little soon?

> KANAKA
> Why? Having second thoughts?

> MONICA
> It's just that, well, I'm taking the detective's exam next month.

> KANAKA
> Shouldn't you be thinking about having babies?

> MONICA
> A baby? You've got to be kidding. My career's just building. I'm sure you can understand that.

> KANAKA
> Maybe I just like being a cop on a beat.

> MONICA
> Well, I want more. I'm going to show those bastards who said a woman couldn't be a detective.

> KANAKA
> Where do I fit in?

                    MONICA
Honey, you fit just fine.

                    KANAKA
Stop it. I'm not your whore.

                    MONICA
Don't talk that way.

Kanaka gets out of the car.

                    KANAKA
This isn't what I want. None of it.

Monica sticks her head out of the window.

                    MONICA
Come back. Darling, all the success in the world means nothing
unless you're beside me. I need you!

Kanaka walks off into the night.

INT. POLICE CAR – MOVING – NIGHT

Cookie drives Monica away from the house.

                    COOKIE
Monica, you okay?

                    MONICA
Of course I am. Strange that the victim had only one testicle
stuffed in his mouth. I believe they usually come in pairs.

                    COOKIE
That's cuz he only had one. I checked. Plenty of meat but only one
potato.

                    MONICA
Cookie, the girl who was murdered at the drive-in. Do you recall
any distinguishing marks or scars?

                    COOKIE
Yes, indeedy. Victim had a hare-lip.

                    MONICA
Precisely. A hare-lip. A common birth defect. The boy at the beach
suffered from the heartbreak of psoriasis, and this young man had
one nut. Cookie, someone out there has a problem with people
who are different.

INT. THE FORREST KITCHEN – DAY

Chicklet and Berdine watch Mrs. Forrest slicing a liverwurst.

> MRS. FORREST
>
> Look at this dull blade. Can't even slice through a sandwich meat.
> If there's one thing I can't stand it's imperfection. There's no room
> in the world for it.

She pulls a knife sharpener out of a drawer and proceeds to sharpen
the blade to perfection. The girls' puzzled expressions are reflected in
the gleaming knife.

EXT. THE BEACH — DAY

Provoloney, Yo Yo, Starcat, Kanaka, and Chicklet are waxing their
surfboards.

> STARCAT
>
> It's just not the same without T.J. and Junior.

> YO YO
>
> I can still picture old T.J. hanging ten off the nose of his Hobie.

> PROVOLONEY
>
> And all that time, he only had one nut. You think you know a
> person.

> STARCAT
>
> Yeah . . . Hey, Kanaka, you think maybe we oughtta cancel the
> luau? You know, out of respect for the dead.

> KANAKA
>
> No way. We gotta commune under the full moon to celebrate our
> main man, King Neptune.

> CHICKLET
>
> They'd want us to have a good time.

> PROVOLONEY
>
> Us? She's saying "us" again.

> KANAKA
>
> Maybe the kid should come. Might be a good mix, like adding
> Coke to rum.

> CHICKLET
>
> Golly, my first luau! I've never been to an orgy before. What do I
> wear?

REAR SCREEN SEQUENCE

Chicklet leads the pack as they ride the waves to the tune of The Esquires' "WHAT A BURN." The girl's been practicing because this time she's able to pull off some amazing stunts, standing on Starcat's shoulders, standing on her hands and doing the splits.

EXT. THE BEACH – DAY

The sun is beginning to set. Starcat holds Chicklet in a brotherly embrace. She melts in his arms. He breaks away from her.

> STARCAT (CONT'D)
> Hey, I gotta split. Gonna be late meeting Marvel Ann. Chicklet, old pal, can you loan me a few bucks to buy something sweet to keep my girl cuddly?

> CHICKLET
> (disappointed)
> Sure.

Chicklet walks away, rolling her eyes.

INT. POLICE STATION – DAY

Monica stands in front of a large bulletin board covered with photographs of the victims. With her is the esteemed psychiatrist, DR. EDWARDS. His moustache and goatee make him look remarkably like Dr. Wentworth in "The Pizza Waitress with Three Heads."

> MONICA
> Frankly Dr. Edwards, in the past I've had little use for you headshrinkers. Inkblot tests, I hate my mother and all that crap. But with this case, I find myself at a loss. I'm told you specialize in the treatment of homicidal maniacs.

> EDWARDS
> Yes but I've never been involved in a criminal investigation.

> MONICA
> Don't worry, you can leave the cops and robbers stuff to me. What I need from you is this. What kind of sicko am I looking for?

> EDWARDS
> It's clear that the perpetrator preys upon the vulnerable unfortunates who the killer deems somehow flawed.

> MONICA
> Give me a profile.

EDWARDS

I'd say the assailant was highly sophisticated yet child-like. Vulnerable but canny.

Monica is deep in thought. Above her head, we SUPER-IMPOSE a shot of Chicklet looking very guilty.

EDWARDS (CONT'D)

Capable of both tenderness and grotesque brutality.

Monica now has a vision of an evil looking Kanaka SUPERIMPOSED over her head.

EDWARDS (CONT'D)

The murderer is highly intelligent yet strangely out of touch with reality.

Monica sees a demonic Mrs. Forrest SUPER-IMPOSE over her head.

EDWARDS (CONT'D)

Sexual yet surprisingly innocent.

Monica now has a vision of a trampy looking Bettina SUPERIMPOSED over her head.

Edwards takes out his pipe and lights it.

EDWARDS (CONT'D)

This individual has an insatiable craving for normalcy. And that, my dear Captain Stark, shall make your investigation all the more difficult.

MONICA

How so?

EDWARDS

Because the killer will do everything in his power to pass as normal. He or she could be anyone.

Monica is deeply perplexed. Above her head is SUPER-IMPOSED the image of a head with the face blurred to obscurity and a large question mark instead of features.

EXT. KANAKA'S SHACK – DAY

Chicklet finds Kanaka outside his shack carving human features into a wooden pole.

CHICKLET

Whatcha doin'?

KANAKA

For the luau. The Pagan God of sex.

CHICKLET

Funny coincidence. Cause that's what I need some advice about. See, there's this girl I know who's friends with this guy but she wants to be more than just friends. What I need to know is, if she puts out, will he respect her?

Kanaka goes inside and Chicklet follows.

INT. KANAKA'S SHACK – DAY

Kanaka grabs a beer out of the cooler.

KANAKA

Kid, lesson number one: don't be sleazy. Nobody wants what they can get too easy. For instance, I've got this lady friend. Haven't seen her in awhile.

CHICKLET

That makes you really miss her,huh?

KANAKA

Uh-huh. Don't even know how to reach her. Name's Ann Bowman. Ring a bell?

CHICKLET

Nope. She live around here?

KANAKA

Real close. It's still sort of a mystery to me what turns her on.

Trying to find the key that will turn Chicklet into Ann Bowman, he bends over pretending to be reaching for something, hoping that this view of his ass will transform Chicklet into Ann.

CHICKLET

Something wrong with your back?

Kanaka, embarrassed, stands up.

KANAKA

I must be out of my gourd. Kid, before I get myself in a jam, you'd better scram.

CHICKLET

Yeah. My mom would be frosted if she knew I was alone with a man in his house. I don't know why. It's not as if you find me even remotely sexy. You probably –

Chicklet focuses on the round life preserver hanging on the wall. Uh-oh, here she goes again. The life preserver becomes animated, changes colors and swirls. Chicklet is seen against a backdrop of ever spinning circles.

Kanaka, sensing something is different about Chicklet, looks closely at her face. She's transformed into the voracious temptress, Ann Bowman.

> KANAKA
>
> Ann? Are you back?

> CHICKLET
> (as Ann)
>
> With a vengeance! I didn't think that little twerp would ever let me in.

> KANAKA
>
> It's circles, isn't it?

> CHICKLET
> (as Ann)
>
> You're a regular Einstein.

> KANAKA
>
> Mistress Ann, I've been a bad boy.

> CHICKLET
>
> And bad boys get spanked! Bad boys get tortured!

> KANAKA
>
> Cowabunga!!!

He rips off his clothes and is wearing underneath a black corselette, panties, garter belt and stockings.

Suddenly, Chicklet switches from "Ann Bowman" into another self, that of the street-wise black teenager, "Tylene."

> CHICKLET
> (as Tylene)
>
> Boy, whatchoo doin' dressed up like a "ho"?

> KANAKA
>
> Ann?

> CHICKLET
> (as Tylene)
>
> Who you be calling Ann? My name is Tylene. Tylene Carmichael Carmel. I work the checkout at the Safeway. It goin' on four-thirty

and my supervisor Miss Feeley she ax me to work overtime. She
think . . .

Kanaka takes out a studded black leather paddle.

> KANAKA
> Bring Ann back! Look what I've got for you.

> CHICKLET
> (as Tylene)
> Back off! I got me a blade. I cut you. I cut you.

> KANAKA
> Forget the paddle! Bad idea!

> CHICKLET
> (as Tylene)
> Don't you mess with me, boy. Don't you even try to –

She instantly returns to being "Ann."

> CHICKLET (CONT'D)
> (as Ann)
> – escape my power. The world has conspired to suppress me, but I
> have risen like a phoenix to claim my birthright. Ann Bowman,
> Dominatrix Empress of the Planet Earth. Catchy, isn't it?

> KANAKA
> Look, I think I've gotten in over my head.

INT. AUGIE'S COFFEE SHOP – DAY

Bettina, her hair covered with a scarf and wearing huge dark glasses,
totters into Augie's in her spike heels, followed by secretary Berdine,
and chief flunkies, Yo Yo and Provoloney.

> BERDINE
> Miss B, Augies does deliver.

> BETTINA
> Berdine, how can I express universal emotions if I don't observe
> how real people live.
> (surveying the room)
> How terribly human.

They sit down in a booth.

> BETTINA (CONT'D)
> We mustn't draw attention to ourselves. We're here to observe.
> Look over there. Brave soul.

RHONDA rolls toward them in her wheelchair.

> BERDINE
>
> She's pretty brave, all right.

> RHONDA
>
> Hello Berdine.

> BERDINE
>
> Hello Rhonda.

> RHONDA
>
> Not alone for a change. Gonna introduce me to your new friends?

> BERDINE
>
> This is Yo Yo and Provoloney.

> RHONDA
>
> Oh, intellectual types.

> BERDINE
>
> And this is uh – this is my cousin Frieda Deefendorfer from Altoona.

> RHONDA
>
> You're not from Altoona. You're Bettina Barnes.

> BETTINA
>
> You're very sweet and very pretty.

> RHONDA
>
> So that is your real voice. I thought maybe they messed with it to make it sound funny.

> BETTINA
>
> Would you care to join us?

> RHONDA
>
> No, I've gotta get going. I've friends coming over for dinner. Berdine, you're not invited. Miss Barnes, I'm a real fan. And, you know, for crummy movies, the camera work must be pretty good. Can't even see those itty bitty lines. Anyway, it's been a thrill. Kisses.

Rhonda wheels away. Bettina, suddenly insecure, picks up a knife from the table and checks her face in the reflection. Pat comes over sensing the carnage.

> PAT
>
> That wheelchair needs an ejector seat. What can I do you for?

I think we need a few more minutes.

Pat turns to Bettina.

PAT

Hon, has anyone ever told you that you're a ringer for that gal who makes all those stinky horror movies?

Reeling from all the insults, Bettina gasps for air.

BETTINA

I need air. Oxygen. I'm suffocating. Have to go outside.

PROVOLONEY

I'll go with you.

BETTINA

No, I must be alone. Don't worry. Just order me a Reuben, fries and a cherry Coke.

She runs out of the coffee shop.

EXT. A STREET CORNER NEAR AUGIES – DAY

Rhonda tries to get her wheelchair over the curb. She looks up and sees a familiar face.

What are you looking at, Asshole?

Her perpetually sneering expression turns to one of fear. POV of the killer, pushing her wheelchair around the corner and into an alley.

RHONDA (CONT'D)

What are you doing? I don't need your stinkin' help. Where the hell are you taking me?

INT. AUGIE'S COFFEE SHOP – DAY

Berdine, Yo Yo and Provoloney are still waiting for Bettina to return. Pat brings them their food.

PAT

Here's your tuna melt and your BLT.
                    (to Provoloney)
You've got the prunes. These oughtta loosen you up. Isn't your friend coming back?

BERDINE

I hope so.

Pat looks toward the door.

Oh, my Lord.

Chicklet as Ann Bowman has entered the coffee shop. She's wearing heavy black eye makeup, draped with a wild red feather boa and smoking from a long cigarette holder.

CHICKLET

Berdine, dahling. It's been ages.

BERDINE

Chicklet?

YO YO

Where'd you find that get up?

CHICKLET

A gift – from an admirer. You think it's too chic for the beach crowd?
(to Pat)
I'm panting for a cocktail. A highball, baby, and hold the fruit.

PAT

You're not even old enough to be smoking.

Pat takes the cigarette out of her holder.

CHICKLET

Peasant, be gone. You're annoying me.

PROVOLONEY

You're on a wild groove.

YO YO

Love your eye makeup. Very Cleopatra.

CHICKLET

Well, I – I.

She wipes her eyelid and sees the black eye makeup on her fingers. She snaps out of it and is Chicklet again.

CHICKLET (CONT'D)

What's this all over my fingers?

She notices the feather boa and cigarette holder.

CHICKLET (CONT'D)

And what's this?

YO YO

I think it's fabulous.

BERDINE

Are you all right?

CHICKLET

Berdine – it's happened again.

PROVOLONEY

What happened?

CHICKLET

I was at Kanaka's and then – Oh God, what's wrong with me?

BERDINE
(covering up)

Nothing's wrong with you. She's just putting you guys on. Ever since we were kids, she's been doing funny voices. Do your Burt Lancaster. "Birdman of Alcatraz."

POLICE SIRENS are heard.

Chicklet and Berdine look panicked.

EXT. THE ALLEY – DAY

Flashing police lights, a small crowd is gathered around something horrific.

Monica and Cookie push their way through the crowd.

COOKIE

Clear a path. Police. All of youse. Ee-vaporate!

As they break through they can see that Rhonda has been savagely decapitated. Her severed head is spinning on the hub of one of the wheels of her wheelchair. In the crowd are Chicklet, Berdine and Bettina.

Monica surveys the grotesque crime scene.

MONICA

A crippled girl. Fits the pattern.

Monica approaches Bettina.

MONICA (CONT'D)

Miss Barnes, why am I getting a feeling of deja vu?

BETTINA

I have a breath mint in my purse, Sweetie. Will that help?

MONICA

It's a strange coincidence that all of your recent personal appearances have been at crime scenes.

BETTINA

Say, is that a crack?

INT. POLICE STATION – MONICA'S OFFICE – DAY

Monica is seated at her desk. Cookie opens the door wide and motions the kids to come in. Yo Yo, Provoloney, and Starcat enter.

MONICA

Fellas, do please sit down.

The guys sit down on a sofa.

MONICA (CONT'D)

I want to talk to you about the murders that have been taking place. I'm concerned that one of you could be the killer's next target.

YO YO

Why us?

MONICA

So far the killer has gone after a girl with a hare-lip, a young lady in a wheelchair, a boy with psoriasis, and another with one testicle. Is there anything about you that the killer could possibly perceive as freakish?

The guys are silent. No one wants to be the first to talk.

MONICA (CONT'D)

Come now. 'Fess up. Everyone has something they'd rather hide.

STARCAT

Since he won't say it, I'll tell you. Provoloney's so constipated, he's in "Ripley's Believe it or Not" for going sixty-seven days without taking a dump.

PROVOLONEY

You want see a freak? Starcat, show her your big toe. The nail fell off and it makes you wanna puke.

MONICA

You guys think this is real funny.

PROVOLONEY

Well, you know, wheelchairs and hare-lips and stuff, kinda cracks ya up.

MONICA

You kids. I just hope some day decent people will no longer find this sort of sick humor a source of comedy. Yo Yo, penny for your thoughts.

YO YO

There's nothing wrong with me.

MONICA

This is for your own protection. Do you feel different in any way?

YO YO

I um – maybe a little . . .

PROVOLONEY
(interrupts)

What are you talking about? You're a hundred per cent normal.

YO YO

I am but sometimes I feel like there's something in me that's kind of – The way I feel toward – I mean, Provoloney and me –

Provoloney freaks out and charges for the door.

PROVOLONEY

I can't believe this! Forget it! I hope the killer knocks us all off!

He storms out of the office.

YO YO

Provoloney!

Yo Yo chases after him. Starcat looks disturbed.

INT. CHICKLET'S BEDROOM – DAY

Chicklet and Berdine sit on Chicklet's bed while listening to "MIGRAINE" by the Hustlers on the record player.

CHICKLET

What exactly did I sound like?

BERDINE

Like an old lady. Like you were thirty.
(imitating her)

Berdine, dahling.

CHICKLET

You won't tell anyone I'm a nutjob, will you?

BERDINE

Of course not. Chicklet Forrest, you are my best friend. I'd keep
your secret forever.

CHICKLET

You'd do that for me?

BERDINE

I'd take a bullet. It makes me feel like the way things used to be,
when it was just the two of us.

The intimacy between the girls is palpable and just when we think
they may actually kiss, Lars, holding a pair of pants, peeks into the
open door.

LARS

Hello girls. Florence, may I ask of you a favor? I wish to wear
these trousers to the luau Saturday night but the button fell off.
I'm not good with the needle. Each time I put my hand in the
pants, I feel a prick.

CHICKLET

Sure thing, Lars.

LARS

Thanks.

Lars leaves. Chicklet closes the door. The girls crack up laughing.

BERDINE

Oh, the luau. I can't wait to hear all about it.

CHICKLET

I'm not going.

BERDINE

But you've got to. You've been canvassing for that invitation all
summer.

CHICKLET

I know. But what if I blow a fuse and short out the entire party?

EXT. NEENIE'S FAMOUS WEINIES – DAY

Chicklet sips her Coke as she walks away from the counter.

CHICKLET (V.O.)
What goes on when I black out? Golly, could I be the nut who's
been butchering all these people? I'll never get into a good school.

She sees Starcat and Marvel Ann sitting at a nearby table. She hides
behind a partition and eavesdrops on them.

MARVEL ANN
You've got to finish college. It's a terrible tragedy seeing all of your
wonderful money-making potential going to waste.

STARCAT
That's parents stuff. Kanaka says I've got the potential to be a
great surfer.

She gets up to leave.

STARCAT (CONT'D)
Where are you going?

MARVEL ANN
I'm mapping out my future and you're not in it. And here, take
back your tacky old ten cent pin.

She tries to unpin it from the side of her bikini bottom.

STARCAT
Let me help you.

MARVEL ANN
Get your hands off me.

STARCAT
Stop moving. I think I can get it.

With a big yank, he pulls off the pin, accidentally ripping the tiny side
of her bikini bottom. The whole thing falls off. Marvel Ann screams
and tries to cover her genitalia.

STARCAT (CONT'D)
Marvel Ann, I'm so sorry.

MARVEL ANN
You did that on purpose. You are a selfish, disgusting, perverted
weirdo and my advice to you is to straighten up, buckle down,
and apply yourself like any other decent, normal Presbyterian!

She runs out of the snack bar.

EXT. A ROCKY PART OF THE BEACH — DAY

Starcat sits down by the rocks. Chicklet joins him.

CHICKLET

Girl trouble?

STARCAT

It's a lot more than that. I'm an extremely complex person with deep-rooted neuroses and anxieties. Why am I telling you this? You're just a kid.

CHICKLET

I'm not just a kid. I'm – how did Kanaka put it? "A luscious voluptuary."

STARCAT

He never said that. Liar.

CHICKLET

He taught me how to surf, didn't he? And he always wants to see me alone. As a matter of fact, I'm headed over to Kanaka's shack later today, for an extremely intimate tete a tete.

She rises and walks away. Starcat catches up to her.

STARCAT

You're just trying to make me jealous.

CHICKLET

Hah! If we were at war with the Soviet Union, I wouldn't even let you into my bomb shelter.

STARCAT

Hey come on. Didn't we call a truce?
You know, you could be a tasty morsel to some wolf.

CHICKLET

Starcat, what do you do with Marvel Ann? I mean, when you're alone.

STARCAT

This is embarrassing, Chicklet.

CHICKLET

Tell me. I need to learn about this stuff.

Lush romantic music underscores this scene. We're moving into heavy "A Summer Place" territory here.

STARCAT

She nestles real close to me.

Chicklet cuddles next to him.

                              CHICKLET
    Kind of like this?

                              STARCAT
    Yeah, sort of like that. I hold her in my arms.

                              CHICKLET
    Like this? And then what do you do?

                              STARCAT
    I kiss the back of her neck.

He gently kisses her neck.

                              CHICKLET
    In the movies, they lie down together. Like over by those rocks.

She takes his hand and drags him over to the rocks. They sit down.

                              STARCAT
    I can't do this with you.

                              CHICKLET
    Pretend I'm Marvel Ann. I need to know about this stuff.

                              STARCAT
    I stroke her arm and she kisses my chest.

Chicklet kisses his chest.

                              CHICKLET
    You take your clothes off, right?

                              STARCAT
    Uh huh. I caress her smooth satiny flesh. It glows in the sunset.
    She gently touches my muscles with her fingertips. She sinks to her
    knees with a look of loving rapture. My erect penis grazes her
    cheek. She slides it in her mouth, cupping my balls with one hand
    and playing with my anus with her finger.

Chicklet screams in revulsion and runs away.

                         STARCAT (CONT'D)
    Chicklet! Chicklet! Come back!

EXT. KANAKA'S SHACK – DAY

Starcat races to Kanaka's shack before Chicklet arrives.

INT. KANAKA'S SHACK – DAY

Kanaka is spray waxing his memorabilia. Starcat bursts in.

STARCAT

Kanaka.

KANAKA

Hold on, Doctor. I don't dig surprise visits.

STARCAT

I wanted to get here before Chicklet.

KANAKA

What's it to you? She's not your chick.

STARCAT

And she shouldn't be yours either. She's only a kid.

KANAKA

That's all you know.

STARCAT

If you've laid a finger on her . . .

KANAKA

Hey, cool out. I've never even touched her. But let me tell ya, she is
off-the-wall. There is more to that Chicklet than meets the old
eyeball. There's like two Chicklets in one.

STARCAT

What are you talking about?

KANAKA

I know it's odd but she's like twins in one bod.

STARCAT

Are you saying she's got a split personality?

KANAKA

Split? One's an angel and the other's a she-devil. Calls herself Ann
Bowman and the screwy thing is I can turn her off and on like a
flashlight.

STARCAT

Do you think this Ann Bowman could be violent?

KANAKA

You tell me.

Kanaka pulls down his pants and turns around. Scratched on his ass
are the words "Ann Bowman lives!"

I hope you put some Bactine on that scratch. Kanaka, I hate to say this but our little Chicklet could be the butcher of Malibu Beach!

Chicklet appears in the doorway.

CHICKLET

Hi.

The two guys jump.

STARCAT

Hey there, Chicklet. We were just um talking about you.

CHICKLET

Checking up on me, huh? Well, if it isn't the Malibu branch of the CIA.

Kanaka takes Chicklet by the arm.

KANAKA

Chicklet, I've been fixing up the place.

Only now do we see that his shack has been redecorated with circular objects; a picture of a bull's-eye, polka dot curtains, a mobile with circular discs.

KANAKA (CONT'D)

What do you think of the new curtains? Lots of circles. I know how you dig them crazy circles. Starcat, I want you to meet the friend I told you about.

STARCAT

You lousy son of a . . .

Starcat punches Kanaka. They fight, knocking over totem poles and tribal shields. Chicklet tries to come between them and for her efforts accidentally gets socked in the kisser. She falls to the floor, unconscious.

KANAKA

Now you've done it, man.

STARCAT

I've done it?

They cradle her in their arms. Chicklet comes to.

CHICKLET

What happened?

LOUD KNOCKING is heard outside the door.

> KANAKA

Who is it?

The door opens and it's Mrs. Forrest. She surveys the scene.

> MRS. FORREST

Dear God.

> KANAKA

Who the hell are you?

> CHICKLET

Mother, what are you doing here?

> MRS. FORREST

Your oboe recital was at four o'clock. Do you even care? To track you down I had to consort with the lowest form of beach scum – only to find you here! Like this!

> STARCAT

Mrs. Forrest, you don't understand.

> MRS. FORREST

Indeed I do. I believe this is what you young people call a "gang bang".

> CHICKLET

Kanaka and Starcat are my friends.

> MRS. FORREST

Florence, please, wait outside.

> CHICKLET

But Mother –

> MRS. FORREST

End of discussion. Just get in the car.

Chicklet scoots out of the shack, humiliated.

> MRS. FORREST (CONT'D)

I'll have you know, I fully intend to press charges. You two had better find yourselves a good lawyer because I'm going to – I'm going to tear your peckers off in that courtroom!

She runs out of the shack.

INT. POLICE STATION – MONICA'S OFFICE – DAY

Monica sits at her desk going over her reports. Cookie enters.

> COOKIE

Captain?

> MONICA

Yes, Cookie.

> COOKIE

I just checked the plates of that Dodge. It's registered under the name Thor Frestur, Mar Vista, California.

> MONICA

Sounds phoney. Like an anagram. Thor Frestur. Put the R before the F, the T in front of the E, and you get Rose H. Toruff. Hmmm. Take the H and move it to the fourth spot and the o to last syllable, Seth R. Ruffort. No, that's not it. Put the R back in the first slot and the F at the top of the last name, and what have you got? Mrs. Ruth Forrest.

INT. THE FORREST KITCHEN – NIGHT

Mrs. Forrest is seated at the kitchen table with a pitcher of manhattans. Rachmaninoff PLAYS in the background. Her perfect hairdo is askew and there's something downright decadent about her.

Lars enters wearing a Hawaiian shirt and lei around his neck.

> LARS

Good evening, Mrs. Forrest.

> MRS. FORREST

Lars, look at you.

> LARS

I'm on my way to the luau. I wanted to ask you, my car is still in the shop. Might I –

> MRS. FORREST

Take the Dodge. Anytime. Never use it.

> LARS

Shall I wait and give Florence a ride?

> MRS. FORREST

I've forbidden her from attending. I had no idea she's been palling around with that disgusting beach trash. Garbage like that ought to be incinerated! Lars, be a lamb and screw the bulb in the overhead. It's been flickering all night and driving me batty.

THE SCREENPLAYS OF CHARLES BUSCH

LARS

But of course, Mrs. Forrest.

MRS. FORREST

Don't you think it's time you called me Ruthie? Climb up on that stool. It should hold your weight. You keep yourself so trim.

Lars climbs up on the stool. Straining to screw in the bulb, his shirt lifts up revealing his muscular stomach.

MRS. FORREST (CONT'D)

I owe you a cocktail for this good turn.

LARS

I don't like the hard liquor.

MRS. FORREST

One little nip ain't gonna kill ya.

She pours from the pitcher and spills some on her blouse.

MRS. FORREST (CONT'D)

Damn it to Hell! Better soak this immediately.

She removes her blouse and tosses it in the sink. She approaches Lars, who is still standing on the stool. She grabs his hips.

MRS. FORREST (CONT'D)

Stool's a little wobbly. Wouldn't want you to fall.

Lars, very uncomfortable, climbs down.

LARS

I think perhaps you require the services of an electrician.

MRS. FORREST

Baby, just screw the goddamn bulb in the socket.

LARS

Mrs. Forrest, I've never seen you like this. This is not you. No, this is not you at all!

Lars, panicked, runs out of the door. Mrs. Forrest finishes her drink, alone.

EXT. THE BEACH – NIGHT

The luau is infull swing. It seems like every SURFER, BEATNIK, CHICK, and KOOK within miles is dancing, drinking from large beer kegs, doing yoga headstands, making out, or lowering themselves under the limbo stick.

A COMBO does a new version of Chubby Checker's 60's classic "The Limbo Rock" – whichever modern rockers we can get to look sufficiently period – Third Eye Blind, Radiohead, Cake. Some band like that.

The music propels all of the kids to dance. They urge Bettina to join them. At first, she declines but the music finally gets to her and hips shaking and hair flinging, she ends up leading the kids in a wild,- choreographed number right out of "Viva Las Vegas".

Marvel Ann makes a big impression with the boys as well and she and Bettina face off in a challenge frug. A V-line of spontaneously choreographed surfers forms behind each of them as they put each other through increasingly complex dance moves.

Marvel Ann stumbles momentarily, tripping up the surfers behind her and causing them to gently trample her. Bettina grooves to the beat as she triumphs over Marvel Ann.

INT. CHICKLET'S BEDROOM – NIGHT

Chicklet is lying on her bed in a deep funk. She hears a tap on the window and is startled to see Berdine's face pressed up against the glass. She lets her in. Berdine lugs in mountain climbing equipment.

> CHICKLET
> How the heck did you get up here?

> BERDINE
> The wonders of literature. "To Everest and Beyond: Mountain Climbing Made Easy." We are going to that luau.

EXT. THE BEACH – NIGHT

Starcat searches through the raucous crowd for Chicklet. He finds Marvel Ann.

> STARCAT
> Marvel Ann.

> MARVEL ANN
> I knew you'd come crawling back.

> STARCAT
> I'm looking for Chicklet. Have you seen her?

> MARVEL ANN
> Yeah. She's at the bottom of this glass.

She throws her drink in his face and stalks away.

He finds Bettina, surrounded by men and autographing their body parts.

> STARCAT
> Bettina, have you seen Chicklet?

> BETTINA
> Come to think of it, I haven't.

Bettina gestures to JOEY, a young man standing beside her.

> BETTINA (CONT'D)
> Starcat, I want you to meet a new friend of mine. This is Joey.

Joey greets Starcat in sign language.

> BETTINA (CONT'D)
> He's deaf. And look, he's got eleven fingers. Isn't that cute?

> STARCAT
> (under his breath)
> Poor sucker doesn't stand a chance in Hell.

EXT. A BEACH COVE – CONTINUOUS

Yo Yo finds a nearly hysterical Provoloney in a small cove just beyond the luau.

> YO YO
> Everything copacetic?

> PROVOLONEY
> Nothing's copacetic. The poi is overcooked. I see no lychee nuts. I ordered lychee nuts and the pineapple's gone bad. You can't make a pu pu platter without pineapple.

Yo Yo grabs him by the shoulders

> YO YO
> Pull yourself together, Provoloney. You're at the breaking point.

> PROVOLONEY
> I can't take the pressure.

Yo Yo has had enough and kisses Provoloney. The two boys kiss passionately. They finally break apart.

> PROVOLONEY (CONT'D)
> Jeeze. My insides are suddenly moving. I um really got to go.

Do what you gotta do. And Provoloney, when you get back, I'll be
waiting for you.

PROVOLONEY
Yo Yo, you're the greatest.

Provoloney winces from the sensation of his bowels finally moving
and runs off. Yo Yo watches his departing figure, blissfully.

EXT. ANOTHER PART OF THE BEACH – CONTINUOUS

Chicklet and Berdine enter the luau. Chicklet is wearing a lovely dress
and looks surprisingly grown-up.

Starcat, taken with her new look, approaches her. Berdine,
diplomatically, steps away.

STARCAT
Chicklet. Wow, you look so –

CHICKLET
Glamorous? Sophisticated? Scrumptious?

STARCAT
Yeah. I don't know how to say this, but you shouldn't be here.

CHICKLET
Oh, I get the picture.

STARCAT
You do?

CHICKLET
Now that Marvel Ann's here, I'm back to being Lassie to your
Timmy. Now get this. I'm going to be the life of this luau, and if
anyone tries to stop me, I'll – I'll kill him.

She walks away, leaving Starcat even more anxious.

Chicklet, defiantly, slides under a limbo pole held by two surfers and
disappears into the crowd.

Lars appears at the luau. A tough-looking punk, WEDGE REILLY,
approaches him and playfully fingers the beads hanging from Lars'
neck. He then removes Lars' glasses and tries them on.

Starcat and Kanaka watch them.

STARCAT
Kanaka, what gives? You know those characters?

KANAKA

I've had the displeasure. Wedge Reilly is out of the big house and the coroner is hurting for slabs. I wonder if the two could be related.

Wedge notices them talking about him.

STARCAT

It looks like they want to start something.

KANAKA

This started a long time ago.

Kanaka decides to check it out. He and Starcat cross over to Wedge.

KANAKA (CONT'D)

Wedge Reilly, so what brings you to our nocturnal celebration?

WEDGE

Just a friendly visit. No need for confrontation.

KANAKA

Wedge, old man, I appreciate the wit. But from trash like you, I take no shit.

WEDGE

Cool, Daddy-o, cool. Over this domain you rule. I'm gonna give you some good advice. To honor King Neptune, you need a virgin sacrifice.

STARCAT

A virgin sacrifice? What the hell's that?

KANAKA

An ancient ritual started in Del Mar in 1952. Forget it, Wedge.

Chicklet overhearing this conversation, joins them.

CHICKLET

What happens to the virgin sacrifice? I mean, what do you to her?

STARCAT

You shouldn't even be here.

CHICKLET

There you go, treating me like a pipsqueak again.

KANAKA

We were gonna do the ritual, but it turns out, we got no virgins.

CHICKLET

Well, I'll do it. I'm a man – I mean, I'm a virgin.

Wedge looks her over, lasciviously.

WEDGE

Oh yeah. Fresh as a salad out of the fridge. You'll do nicely.

STARCAT

I won't let you.

Berdine, nearby, has overheard them.

BERDINE

Please, Chicklet. Don't. It's an existential fate worse than death.

WEDGE

Don't let your pal spoil a night you'll never forget.

CHICKLET
(gulps)

Let the ritual begin! I do have a few conditions. First of all, no blindfolds and –

Before she can finish, two of Wedge's henchmen carry her off to prepare her for the ritual.

TIME CUT

EXT. THE BEACH – NIGHT

Starcat and Kanaka wait for Chicklet to reappear.

STARCAT

What's going on back there?

Drumbeats are heard and Chicklet, draped in exotic flowers and beads, is carried in on a litter held aloft by Wedge's followers.

Provoloney, Bettina and Yo Yo watch the procession in wonder.

YO YO

Is that Chicklet?

PROVOLONEY

She's got more garnish on her than my grandmother's antipasto.

BETTINA

She has clothes on. That's more than I got back in Altoona.

Wedge, wearing a headdress, begins the ritual.

King Neptune, to you we offer the ring of fate. In other words, scum bags, form a circle!

The kids all form a circle around Chicklet.

KANAKA
(panicked)
Um – no circles. That's not the way we do things around here.

Indeed, the formation of the "circle" triggers Chicklet's alternate personality and she transforms into Ann Bowman, throwing her head back and laughing with abandon.

CHICKLET
(as Ann)
Dance! Fools! Dance!

WEDGE
Hey, that ain't the way a virgin should act.

CHICKLET
(as Ann)
Kiss my ass, flunkie. I'm calling the shots now. Put me down from this thing.

The boys lower the litter to the ground.

CHICKLET (CONT'D)
(as Ann)
Where's my whip? Who's got my goddam whip?

Berdine tries to cover up for Chicklet's personality change.

BERDINE
Now Chicklet's going to do some impressions. Do your Zsa Zsa.

CHICKLET
(as Ann)
Don't touch me.

Chicklet grabs a beer bottle from Lars, who's standing nearby. She breaks it against a large totem pole and threatens them all with the jagged piece of glass.

WEDGE
That's one flaked out chick.

CHICKLET
(as Ann)

I'm no chick. I'm a goddess! And the first thing I'm going to sacrifice are your balls, sonny.

Wedge, freaked out, runs away from her. She chases after him till she is subdued by Starcat and Kanaka.

At this moment, Mrs. Forrest arrives on the scene with Captain Monica, Cookie and other back-up cops.

MRS. FORREST

There! Officers! Those men seduced my daughter!

Starcat tries to wrestle the jagged glass away from Chicklet.

STARCAT

Your daughter is mentally ill.

MRS. FORREST

She's not sick! She's not sick!

Chicklet as Ann breaks away from Starcat and Kanaka.

CHICKLET
(as Ann)

It's true. I am hardly the lunatic they're painting me to be. I am utterly in control.

STARCAT

You are merely a delusion of Chicklet Forrest that enables her to express anger and rage.

CHICKLET
(as Ann)

Fancy phrases. And a big basket.

STARCAT

I'm going to place you under hypnosis and through the technique of past regression get to the root of the trauma, the guilt complex, that fragmented Chicklet's personality.

MRS. FORREST

I can't allow this. He doesn't know what he's doing.

PROVOLONEY

He's had three semesters of psych at Northwestern.

MONICA

It's either that or an icepick lobotomy. Starcat, proceed.

Starcat removes the Teekee pendant from around his neck and waves it in front of Chicklet's eyes.

> STARCAT
> You're feeling tired, drowsy. You want to close your eyes.

> MRS. FORREST
> Someone stop this madness!

> CHICKLET
> (as Ann)
> Oh, shut your hole. Go on, darling Doctor Starcat.

> STARCAT
> I want to talk to Chicklet.

> CHICKLET
> It's hard. I feel so far away. I can't –

Suddenly she transforms into a radio traffic reporter.

> CHICKLET (CONT'D)
> – travel down the Hollywood freeway. Be prepared for –

She switches to a Spanish language station and then suddenly bursts into an operatic aria from *La Boheme*.

> YO YO
> What's going on?

> STARCAT
> It's a bad connection.

Chicklet flips back into herself, albeit as a young child.

> CHICKLET
> Help me.

> STARCAT
> Chicklet, is that you?

> CHICKLET
> Uh huh.

> STARCAT
> How old are you?

> CHICKLET
> Seven and a half. I don't like this place.

Where are you?

FLASHBACK SEQUENCE

INT. A HOTEL ROOM — DAY

Chicklet flashes back to the past and sees herself as a little girl holding her younger brother's hand. They open the door to their mother's bedroom.

Mrs. Forrest is seen as a beautiful and very sexy young woman wearing only a slip. She's in the arms of a SAILOR. She looks up and sees the children.

> MRS. FORREST
> Look who's here. We've got visitors.
> Curtsey Florence like I taught you.

The little girl curtsies.

> LITTLE FLORENCE
> Mama, we're ready to go to the movies.

> MRS. FORREST
> Oh darling, I'm so sorry. We're gonna have to skip the picture.

> LITTLE FLORENCE
> But you promised.

> MRS. FORREST
> Mama's got to do her bit for the boys serving our nation. You and Frankie sit in the living room and listen to the radio.
> (to the sailor)
> Sugar, I don't even know your name.
> He murmurs his name in her ear.

> MRS. FORREST (CONT'D)
> Pleased to meet you, Johnny. My name's Ann. Ann Bowman.

EXT. THE BEACH — NIGHT

Back in the present. Chicklet's face fills the screen.

> CHICKLET
> I was so angry. I wanted to hurt her. I took Frankie across the street to the playground.

EXT. A PLAYGROUND — DAY

The flashback continues. The child Florence and Frankie walk toward the swings.

> CHICKLET (V.O.)
> Please don't make me go on.

> STARCAT (V.O.)
> You gotta. What happened next?

Frankie gets on the swing and little Florence begins to push him.

> CHICKLET (V.O.)
> He kept asking me to push him harder and harder until he was soaring into the clouds. Then Frankie said, "Make me go round the world."

The little girl gives her brother an enormous push and amazingly the swing goes around in a full circle. The effect is magical until the little boy lets go and flies off the swing. Like a cherub, the little boy flies through the clouds.

The young Mrs. Forrest runs into the playground just in time to witness the child fall. Tight close-up as she SCREAMS.

EXT. THE BEACH – NIGHT

Chicklet, reliving the moment, weeps in hysterics. Starcat holds her.

> CHICKLET
> I did it! I did it! I killed him!

Mrs. Forrest finally speaks up.

> MRS. FORREST
> When Florence lost her memory, I took it as a blessing from God. I vowed to create a new life for us. I changed my name, moved to a new city.

> CHICKLET
> Mother, hold me.

Chicklet and her mother embrace.

Bettina, transfixed by this tale, steps forward.

> BETTINA
> That's the most exciting story idea I've heard in years. This is the project that could showcase my talent as a great dramatic actress.

> MRS. FORREST
> A story?

A surfer chick with a split personality. I see a hit Broadway play and I'll sew up the movie rights.
(to Chicklet)
Honey, I want to option this property and believe me, I'll pay top dollar.

STARCAT

Bettina, do you think you're ready to tackle such a complex role?

BETTINA

I don't think! I feel! I know this girl! I am Chicklet!!

CHICKLET

I hate missing your opening night but I'll be in a loony bin for the criminally cuckoo.

MONICA

Not so fast, Chicklet. I wouldn't model that straight jacket just yet.

CHICKLET

But if I didn't butcher all those people, who did?

MONICA

Someone so tormented for being an outsider, that she's compelled to destroy others who don't "fit in".

Monica moves over to Mrs. Forrest.

MONICA (CONT'D)

Mrs. Forrest, you're under arrest.

CHICKLET

Oh no! It can't be true!

Cookie places handcuffs on Mrs. Forrest.

MRS. FORREST

What are you doing? This is a dreadful mistake.

COOKIE

Come on, Sister. You're goin' places.

Cookie tries to steer her to the squad car.

MRS. FORREST
(protesting wildly)
Get your hands off me! I'm innocent, I tell you. I'm innocent!

Several COPS try to get Mrs. Forrest into the squad car. She puts up a fierce struggle, biting and kicking.

> COOKIE
> Cut her off at the ankles.

Mrs. Forrest gets her legs in a stranglehold around a post as the men and Cookie try to pull her away.

> MRS. FORREST
> I'm not movin'! Just try and get me, Pigwoman!

> COOKIE
> Lady, you're gettin' me steamed.

Cookie pulls her off the post and handcuffs her.

> CHICKLET
> Please, don't hurt her!

> MRS. FORREST
> You won't get away with this! Motherfucking, cocksuckers!

They load her into the backseat of the squad car. Monica and Cookie get in the front seat and drive off.

Starcat puts his arm around Chicklet's shoulders.

> CHICKLET
> My mother a murderess. What next?

She sees Berdine, looking lost and forlorn.

> CHICKLET (CONT'D)
> Berdine, did I hurt you? I'm so sorry.

> BERDINE
> I thought by making excuses for you I was being a best friend. I should've gotten you help. I stink rotten eggs.

Berdine bursts into tears. Chicklet embraces her.

> STARCAT
> We've got to get you both home.

Among the crowd is Joey, the deaf boy with eleven fingers. He catches Berdine's eye and winks at her, misfit to misfit. Berdine, wipes her nose and considers her options.

> BERDINE
> Actually, I think I'd like to stay a bit longer.

Lars, who has been a part of this group, steps forward.

> LARS
>
> I can take Florence home.

> CHICKLET
>
> Lars, you sure picked one heck of an American family to shack up with.

> LARS
>
> I'm not worried.

> CHICKLET
> (to Starcat)
>
> How can I ever thank you?

> STARCAT
>
> You being Chicklet again's all the thanks I need. Believe me, one's enough.

Starcat leans intoward Chicklet. She looks up at him, ready to receive his kiss. He hesitates, then:

> LARS
>
> Shall we go?

> CHICKLET
> (to Starcat)
>
> Guess this is goodnight.

Chicklet, hesitant to leave, turns back and exchanges one last longing look with Starcat. She and Lars walk off toward the parking lot.

INT. LARS' CAR – MOVING – NIGHT

Chicklet looks out the window as Lars drives them home.

> LARS
>
> Florence, this must be the worst thing that's ever happened to you.

> CHICKLET
>
> It's definitely up there in the top ten.

> LARS
>
> Your mother couldn't help herself. In her own way, she believed she was helping those poor, sick people.

> CHICKLET
>
> I hope you don't mind but I'm not really in the mood for conversation.

LARS
I understand completely . . .
(long pause)
Still, I was surprised to learn of your deep psychological problems.
I always thought of you as a well-adjusted typical American girl.
Almost boring, really.

CHICKLET
Sorry to disappoint you.

LARS
There is so much ugliness in the world. Can't there be anyone who
is utterly perfect?

Chicklet is becoming increasingly nervous at this turn in the
conversation. She spots a 24-hour coffee shop up ahead.

CHICKLET
Gee, all those revelations tonight have made me famished. How's
about stopping over there for a quick bite?

LARS
I think not.

EXT. BETTINA'S DECK – NIGHT

The luau is over. Starcat, Kanaka, and Berdine help Bettina clean up.

STARCAT
Psychologically, it just doesn't jibe. It can't be Mrs. Forrest.

BETTINA
Poor Chicklet. At least she's not alone. It's a good thing she has
Lars with her.

STARCAT
Yeah. Lars . . . Bettina, do you still have that photo of the Elkins
family?

BETTINA
You mean the ones who were murdered?

BERDINE
I put it in the credenza.

INT. BETTINA'S LIVING ROOM – NIGHT

Berdine hands Starcat the glass-framed photograph.

INSERT: Photo of the Elkins family. Ten-year-old Larry is seated in the middle.

Starcat takes a black marker pen out of his pocket and draws on the glass. The others watch him with confusion.

> KANAKA
> Starcat, what are you doing?

INSERT: The photograph. Starcat has drawn a large pair of glasses and a flattop crewcut on Larry. It looks amazingly like Lars.

Bettina drops the picture, shattering the glass. The Elkins family are trapped in a spider's web of cracked glass.

INT. LARS' CAR – MOVING – NIGHT

Chicklet is perched to jump out but they make every light. As they pass by the drive-in theater, Chicklet slams her foot on the brakes. Lars tries to overpower her but she manages to jump out of the still moving car.

EXT. OUTSIDE THE DRIVE-IN – NIGHT

Chicklet stumbles to her feet as Lars screeches the car to a halt. She surveys the scene and runs toward a small hole in the fence where kids sneak into the show.

Lars exits the car, carrying a large knife, and chases after her.

Lars looks around the deserted drive-in. He has dropped his "Lars" accent and speaks in pure Americanese.

> LARS
> Why are you running away from me? I only want to help you.

He moves toward the concession stand.

BY THE CONCESSION STAND

Chicklet crouches behind the condiment island, terrified. She hears FOOTSTEPS approaching, then stop.

She looks up to see Lars looming over her. Chicklet SCREAMS and jumps back.

> LARS (CONT'D)
> Could you pass the mustard?

> CHICKLET
> Lars, what happened to your accent?

LARS
I don't need it. I can finally be myself. Call me Larry.

CHICKLET
As in . . . Elkins?

Lars takes out his knife.

LARS
Pleased to meet you. Unfortunately, this is also goodbye.

He moves closer. Something in Chicklet clicks and she's transformed into Tylene.

CHICKLET
(as Tylene)
You best be backin' off.

LARS
Huh?

CHICKLET
(as Tylene)
You a nut. Gimme that knife. I'm axing you nicely. Gimme that thing.

LARS
I'll give you the knife.

He rushes toward her. With great expertise, Chicklet (as Tylene) wrestles the knife out of Lars' hands.

CHICKLET
(as Tylene)
You goin' down, Fuck Face.

He fights her for the knife and she stabs it into his shoulder. He sinks to his knees. Chicklet returns to her normal self.

CHICKLET (CONT'D)
(stunned)
Criminy.

Chicklet runs away as Lars/Larry pulls the knife out of his shoulder.

EXT. THE ROAD OUTSIDE THE DRIVE-IN – NIGHT

As Starcat's car drives by, Berdine's voice is heard.

BERDINE
There's the Dodge. Pull over! They must be in the drive-in!

EXT. DRIVE-IN – NIGHT

Larry chases Chicklet to the corner of the drive-in, down by the screen.

Chicklet looks for an escape and sees a ladder of footholds going up the side of the enormous screen. With no other way out, she starts climbing. Lars follows her. Midway up the ladder, Chicklet stops and speaks to Lars.

> CHICKLET
> How could you do that to your own family?

> LARRY
> You're just like all the others. No one understands.

> CHICKLET
> No, try me. I can be very perceptive.

> LARRY
> You can't possibly know what it's like to grow up in a house of freaks. My mother was blind. My father was deaf, and my sisters were midgets. They had to die so I could be free.

> CHICKLET
> So why kill me? I'm your pal. I'm the one who fixed your pants.

> LARRY
> And now I'm gonna fix you.

Chicklet continues to climb up the ladder, closely followed by Lars.

EXT. OUTSIDE THE DRIVE-IN – NIGHT

Starcat, Berdine, Yo Yo, and Provoloney jump out of the car and try to squeeze themselves through the front gate of the drive-in.

They pause for a moment when they see a police car pulling up.

EXT. DRIVE-IN – NIGHT

Chicklet continues climbing up the side of the movie screen, followed closely behind by Lars.

EXT. THE DRIVE-IN SWITCH BOX – NIGHT

Cookie finds the electrical switch box, pulls the switch, and the drive-in is lit up.

Starcat looks up at the screen and sees Chicklet and Lars climbing up the side.

Hey, look over there!

EXT. LANDING – NIGHT

Chicklet reaches a small landing at the top of the screen. Larry is in hot pursuit.

Chicklet runs to the far end of the landing, hoping to find a ladder going down, but there is nothing. She runs back to the other side and meets up with Larry.

> LARRY
> Alone at last. I've got you now just the way I want you.

Grabbing Chicklet's arms, he gets her down on her back. Chicklet transforms into Ann Bowman, temptress, barracuda.

> CHICKLET
> (as Ann)
> You pathetic little worm. No man conquers Ann Bowman.

> LARRY
> What?

Chicklet knees Lars in the groin. He falls back and she gets up.

> CHICKLET
> (as Ann)
> You're weak. You disgust me.

She spits in his face. Larry backs away from her.

> CHICKLET (CONT'D)
> (as Ann)
> You like being humiliated, don't you?

> LARRY
> Help me!!

Starcat yells from below.

> STARCAT
> Chicklet!

Chicklet hears Starcat and is immediately shaken out of being Ann Bowman.

> CHICKLET
> Starcat?

Larry senses that Chicklet is no longer Ann Bowman.

LARRY

    The bitch is gone. Now so are you.

He raises the knife, about to plunge it into her, when a SHOT rings out.

A gun-toting Captain Monica Stark stands at the end of the landing, aiming at Larry.

MONICA

    Put down the knife!

LARRY

    Make me!

Larry moves toward Monica and she fires again, shooting him squarely in the chest. He falls off the landing and lands with a THUD at the bottom of the screen. Larry Elkins is dead at last.

Chicklet and Captain Monica look down at him.

CHICKLET

    Poor Larry.

MONICA

    That's the end of that.

EXT. DRIVE-IN – NIGHT

Chicklet descends from the ladder on the side of the screen, falling into Starcat's arms. She notices the circular sign for the drive-in slowly revolving.

CHICKLET

    The circle goes round and I'm still me.

STARCAT

    You're cured.

Monica also comes down the ladder and is surprised to find herself in Kanaka's arms.

MONICA

    I remember that grip.

KANAKA

    Feels good?

MONICA

    Feels real good.

Kanaka lands her on her feet.

MONICA (CONT'D)
Wanna wrestle?

KANAKA

For the championship.

MONICA

Let's get outta here.

Monica takes Kanaka's hand and they walk off together with the erotic anticipation of wild new times.

EXT. OUTSIDE THE DRIVE IN — NIGHT

Chicklet and Starcat climb through the hole in the fence.

STARCAT

Sure are a lot of twisted souls out there. Maybe I should be a psychiatrist.

CHICKLET

You'd be tops – I'm proof of that.

STARCAT

I'd have to go back to school.

CHICKLET

And leave everything behind?

STARCAT

Not everything. Chicklet, I was wondering . . . will you wear my pin?

CHICKLET

Will I ever!

She jumps into his arms and kisses Starcat. He picks her up and spins her around. He puts her down and they walk off into the night.

T.J. (O.S.)

Wake up, Florence! Wake up!

INT. THE WARD OF AN INSANE ASYLUM — DAY

Chicklet wakes up, dazed. This whole thing and I mean the WHOLE movie has been her dream. T.J. and Junior are orderlies.

CHICKLET

I must've been dreaming.

JUNIOR

Time for your treatment.

Chicklet routinely rises from her slumber and allows them to escort her out, still wearing her hospital gown.

INT. ELECTRIC SHOCK TREATMENT ROOM – DAY

Chicklet lays on a gurney as Junior moistens a pair of electrodes with clear jelly. He places the electrodes on her temples and nods to the nurse manning the controls.

Chicklet cranes her neck to see that the nurse is none other than Rhonda!

> CHICKLET
> You were in my dream. And you were there.

T.J. places a plastic retainer in her mouth that shuts her up.

> RHONDA
> We dream many foolish things when we are ill. Kisses.

With venomous glee, Rhonda places the electrodes on Chicklet's temples, sending Chicklet into convulsions.

CAMERA TRUCKS BACK to show that the entire film we've been watching is on the screen of a drive-in theater. The year is 1966.

EXT. DRIVE-IN MOVIE – NIGHT

A 1966 Mustang convertible. In the front seat, a young COUPLE watch the credits roll for *Psycho Beach Party*.

> BOY
> So it was all her dream? What a gyp!

> GIRL
> It's based on a true story. I'm just glad that creepy Ann Bowman's locked up for good.

Chicklet as Ann Bowman suddenly emerges from the back seat, wielding a knife.

> CHICKLET
> (as Ann)
> Don't be so sure, dahling.

With manic ferocity, she goes in for the kill.

FADE OUT.

ROLL END CREDITS.

CREDITS

FLORENCE "CHICKLET" FORREST	Lauren Ambrose
STARCAT	Nicholas Brendon
LARS/LARRY	Matt Kesslar
CAPTAIN MONICA STARK	Charles Busch
YO YO	Nick Cornish
PROVOLONEY	Andrew Levitas
MARVEL ANN	Amy Adams
RHONDA	Kathleen Robertson
T.J.	Nathan Bexton
JUNIOR	Buddy Quaid
COOKIE	Jenica Bergere

Written by	Charles Busch
Based on the play *Psycho Beach Party* by Charles Busch	
Directed by	Robert Lee King
Cinematography by	Arturo Smith
Produced by	New Oz Productions
Producer	Virginia Biddle
Producer	Diane Cornell
Line producer	Jon Gerrans
Executive Producer	John Hall
Producer	Marcus Hu
Co-executive producer	Jeff Melnick
Producer	Victor Syrmis

Die, Mommie, Die!

EXT. CEMETERY – DAY –

1967, A sunny afternoon in Los Angeles. A woman is seen from the back, walking through the very quiet cemetery. The woman is ANGELA ARDEN SUSSMAN. She is the wife of a famous Hollywood producer. However, once she had a brilliant career as a recording star. We cannot see her face, but one can tell by her clothes and carriage that she's a figure of glamour and stature, strength and vulnerability.

Another woman, a FAN (50's), recognizes her and moves swiftly toward her carrying a beautiful bouquet of flowers.

> FAN
> Miss Arden? You are Angela Arden?

Angela turns around and for the first time we see her beautiful face; the face of a star.

> FAN (CONT'D)
> Miss Arden, I don't want to disturb you but I'd love for you to have these flowers. They're from my garden.

> ANGELA
> Aren't they intended to be lain on a loved one's grave?

> FAN
> I brought them for my late husband but Percy would understand. He was also a big Angela Arden fan.

> ANGELA
> Then I accept them with deep gratitude from both you and Percy.

> FAN
> I wish you'd sing again. We need your kind of music. Real music. Not that vile rock and roll. Do you listen to your old records?

Angela's face tightens. That innocent remark has hit some very raw nerve.

> ANGELA
> No. Never. I really must go.

Angela leaves the fan and heads toward her destination. Credits begin.

DIE, MOMMIE, DIE   99

EXT. CEMETERY – DAY –

Passing by elaborate monuments bearing the names of Tyrone Power and Cecil B. DeMille, at last, Angela stops in front of a very small and modest marker.

INSERT

The gravestone. It reads "Barbara Arden, Beloved Sister, The Song is you, 1922–1954."

INT. A THEATRE – NIGHT

FLASHBACK

1939, ANGELA and BARBARA, age 17, are seen from the back, singing in front of a microphone. The blinding footlights totally obscure the audience.

END OF FLASHBACK

EXT. CEMETERY – DAY

Angela takes a rose from out of the bouquet and gently places it on the grave. The expression on her face is ambiguous. It is clear that her relationship to the deceased was a complex one.

EXT. CEMETERY PARKING LOT – DAY

A very handsome man, somewhat younger than she, TONY PARKER, is waiting for her in front of a car at the curb.

> TONY
> Where'd you get the posies?

> ANGELA
> Would you believe it, a fan?

> TONY
> And here you thought you were a forgotten old lady.

Angela winces at his facetious remark.

EXT. CEMETERY ENTRANCE – DAY

Tony and Angela's sports car pulls out of the cemetery.

INT. TONY'S CAR, DRIVING – DAY

Tony turns on the car radio and an easy-listening instrumental version of one of Angela's big hits is playing.

They don't write 'em like this anymore. A lost art. Didn't you record this once?

Angela stares enigmatically in space, lost in memory.

INT. A TELEVISION VARIETY SHOW SET – NIGHT – B & W

1954, Angela is seen belting out the same song in front of a simple curtain on a television variety show. The black and white photography should have the feel of an early TV kinescope. The credits continue to roll.

We pull back to reveal that the image is on a television screen in a darkened room.

We pull further back to reveal that the image is being watched by a silhouetted woman smoking a cigarette.

EXT. THE SUSSMAN HOME – DAY

The exterior of the beautiful Beverly Hills home of producer Sol P. Sussman and his wife, Angela Arden Sussman.

INT. THE SUSSMAN LIVING ROOM – DAY

The Sussman home is opulent but oddly impersonal. It's a battlefield for a family at war. The devoted housekeeper, BOOTSIE, mid-western, neat as pin, no nonsense, and briskly maternal, is busy vacuuming. Sussman's beautiful but troubled daughter, EDITH (21) runs down the very grand stairway.

> EDITH
> Bootsie, he's here! Turn that thing off!

> BOOTSIE
> Beg your pardon?

Edith shuts off the vacuum cleaner.

> EDITH
> How's my hair? He doesn't like when I tease it too much.

> BOOTSIE
> The hairdo's fine but that mini-dress is two inches shy of giving away the entire candy counter.

> EDITH
> Oh, he'll complain like Hell but you'll see – he'll never take his eyes off my legs.

> BOOTSIE

As my Grandmother Newton used to say, "Men are like Halloween pumpkins, they may look different but inside they're all the same mush."

Edith violently twists Bootsie's arm.

> EDITH

Take that back! Take it back!!

> BOOTSIE

Let me go. You're breakin' my arm.

> EDITH

He's not like other men. He's an original. For God sakes, Bootsie, you're talking about my father!

Edie is gravely disappointed when her mother and Tony enter the house.

> ANGELA

Hello, darling. My, don't you look delicious. New dress?

> EDITH

Uh huh. Daddy's favorite color.

> TONY

Suits you just fine, kiddo.

Bootsie, disapproving of the slight sexual innuendo in Tony's remark, takes the vacuum cleaner and exits to the kitchen. Angela arranges the flowers in a vase.

> ANGELA

It's such a sunny day. One could almost walk around nude.

> EDITH

Mother, you would.

> ANGELA

There's nothing wrong with nudity. Tony frequently visits a nudist colony at Big Sur.

> TONY

Feels good letting everything hang in the breeze.

> EDITH

That's revolting.

ANGELA

Darling daughter, you sound like a square from Squaresville.

EDITH

Square to you because I don't sleep around with every delivery boy or valet parking attendant.

ANGELA

You're affecting a rather severe tone, young lady.

EDITH

Severe to a woman who rubs cocoa butter on Sammy Davis Junior.

ANGELA

Sammy is a cherished friend of this family. I refuse to justify my actions to you.

EDITH

Because you can't.

ANGELA

Oh, Edie, why must we be forever at each other's throats?

TONY

Can't you try and meet your mother half way? She's a good egg.

ANGELA

There's no use talking to her when she's in a mood. Tony, be a dear. Fix me something nice and cool and meet me in the garden.

Angela takes her coat and scarf and leaves the room. Tony crosses toward the kitchen.

INT. THE SUSSMAN KITCHEN – DAY

Tony, followed by Edith, enters the kitchen. He opens the refrigerator, finds the vodka, tonic water, and some lime and fixes the drinks. Edie sits on top of the sink.

EDITH

It's been so considerate of you keeping my mother company while my dad's been in Spain.

TONY

I'm glad I've been able to entertain her.

EDITH

As a student of psychology, I wonder what you could possibly see in my mother besides her frequently opened checkbook?

TONY

She's a wonderful gardener. How long have you felt so kindly toward your mother?

EDITH

I guess deep down I've always known the truth about her.

TONY

What truth?

EDITH

I don't have to tell you anything. You're not my shrink.

Edith turns to leave. Tony grabs her arm.

TONY

What secret did you learn? Why do you hate her so?

EDITH

I hate her because she's – because she's a money-grubbing selfish bitch who ruined my father's life. And she's a promiscuous slut who spends my father's hard-earned money on trash like you.

TONY

That's not good enough.

EXT. THE GARDEN – DAY

Angela is seated in the garden. Tony joins her from the house.

TONY

Quite a picture. Angela Arden surrounded by her prize-winning Angela Arden roses.

ANGELA

I seem to have a green thumb for everything but raising children.

TONY

It's just a phase, Angie. All kids go through it.

ANGELA

When did it start? When did it all go wrong?

Angela rises from her chair and pensively looks out at the view.

TONY

After your sister Barbara died?

ANGELA
(tenses)

Why should you say that?

TONY

Sometimes a death in the family, the death of a beloved aunt, can be a traumatic experience for a child.

ANGELA

Perhaps something did happen that summer. One can feel the memory lingering like smog over the canyon. Whatever it was, I've paid for it dearly.
(vulnerably)
What about you, Tony? Have I paid enough for you?

TONY

Stop it! Stop it right there. That's not funny. You know you're my girl.

ANGELA

Am I? Tony, you ask me to throw away everything safe and secure for a man whose reputation is that of a highly paid gigolo.

TONY

I've always been the sort of guy people spread rumors about. Hell, there was a certain rumor about me that made you reach for the phone in the first place.

She starts to slap him but he catches her arm.

ANGELA

Who are you, Tony Parker? You've slipped into my life as easily as vermouth into a glass of gin. Quickly and just a bit too smooth. Your life is a locked file cabinet of dark, ugly secrets.

Tony grabs her violently.

TONY

What have you heard?

ANGELA

I have it on excellent authority, by way of every hairburner in West Hollywood, that the favors you've received were not only courtesy of the ladies but les garcons as well.

TONY

Get this straight. I'm no fag. I've torn men apart for saying less.

He holds her tightly. She's instantly remorseful.

ANGELA

Listen to us. We were nearly arguing. I've never desired any man as I've desired you.

They kiss. Suddenly, they hear Edie shouting from inside.

> EDITH
> (from inside)
He's here! Daddy's home!

INT. THE SUSSMAN LIVING ROOM — DAY

SOL SUSSMAN has come home. He's a movie mogul in his late fifties, a big aggressive personality masking an essential darkness of character. Edie has her arms around his neck.

> SOL
How's my little girl?

> EDITH
Missing you.

Angela and Tony enter.

> ANGELA
Welcome home, Sol.

> SOL
Tony Parker, what brings you here?

> TONY
I drove Mrs. Sussman to visit her sister's grave.

> SOL
Angie was a perfectly good driver until her sister died. Overnight, she developed a phobia about it.

> TONY
Your sister died in a car accident?

> EDITH
No, from an overdose of pills.

Two identical white puppies scamper in and play at Angela's feet. She bends down to snuggle with them.

> ANGELA
Ah, the little darlings. Sol, they're so happy you're home.

> SOL
They're faking it. I'm sure they've got an angle just like everyone else.

Angela gets Sol's "dig," but continues nuzzling the dogs.

Tony bends down to stroke the puppies.

> TONY
>
> They really are identical, aren't they?

> ANGELA
>
> None of God's creations are entirely alike.

Sol is compelled to break up the intimacy between Angela and Tony.

> SOL
>
> So, Tony, how's the acting career? Still dry?

> TONY
>
> I'm holding out. It's not easy finding another TV series with the range and class of *Squad Car Thirteen*. I should get back to the club. I have to give a tennis lesson to a very spoiled ten-year-old named Gwendolyn. Mr. Sussman, it's good having you home.

Tony exits through the front door. Angela picks up the dogs and carries them to the sofa.

> ANGELA
>
> Sol, was your trip successful?

> SOL
>
> It used to be easy raising money for American pictures in Europe. Now it's dried up like a plate of blintzes in the Sahara.

> ANGELA
> (to Edith)
>
> Sweetie, I think these angels need to be walked.

> EDITH
>
> Translation: Get the Hell out of here so I can be a shrew to your father in private. I'll go, Mother, but I'll be back.

Edith takes the dogs and exits the house. Sol fixes himself a drink.

> SOL
>
> My God, I'm proud of that kid. She is my legacy.

> ANGELA
>
> Sol, so much has happened since you've been gone. I've received an offer to sing in New York.

> SOL
>
> At a nightclub?

ANGELA

No, at a resort in the Catskills.

SOL

How much are they paying you?

ANGELA

We haven't worked out all the details but –

SOL

When will you be leaving?

ANGELA

By the end of the week. The top arrangers and musicians are all in New York. It's all tremendously exciting.

Not wanting to continue this discussion, Angela heads up the stairs.

INT. ANGELA'S BEDROOM – DAY

Sol enters just as Angela has removed her dress. Standing in her slip, she grabs her robe and puts it on.

SOL

You're a rotten liar.

ANGELA

I beg your pardon.

SOL

A New York gig? Nobody would hire you to sing at a dogfight. Not with that wobble.

ANGELA

That's not true. I've been practicing every day with my vocal coach. I no longer crack on that high F over middle C. Now if you'll excuse me, I intend to soak in a hot tub and prefer not to be disturbed.

She moves toward the bathroom.

INT. BATHROOM – DAY

CONTINUOUS

Sol follows Angela into the bathroom. She runs the bath.

SOL

I know why you're so eager to get to New York and it ain't to sing at any bar mitzvahs. You've got a lover. And he's rented a townhouse for you both in Greenwich Village. Care to know the floor plan?

ANGELA

No. Though I am mildly curious to hear the identity of my secret paramour.

SOL

Does the name Tony Parker ring a bell?

ANGELA
(laughing)

Tony? Tony Parker?

SOL

Don't you dare laugh.

ANGELA

But really, it's so amusing. Me run off with Tony, a failed TV actor and a notorious lothario?

SOL

Tony Parker's known to have the biggest cock west of the San Andreas Fault. I should've known a tramp like you would come begging for it.

ANGELA

I will not remain here to be insulted.

She leaves the bathroom.

INT. ANGELA'S BEDROOM – DAY

CONTINUOUS

As Angela crosses to the bureau, Sol pushes her down on the bed.

SOL

You're not going anywhere. I had a detective follow you. He's taken pictures. Pictures that made even a hard-boiled gumshoe reach for a Pepto-Bismol.

Sol takes a folder out of his briefcase, removes the 8 × 10 photos, and hands them to Angela.

ANGELA'S POV. A close-up of three lurid black and white photos of a nude Angela and Tony engaged in mind-boggling Kama Sutra-like sexual poses.

ANGELA

I'd say these are certainly grounds for divorce?

SOL

Never. I'm sentencing you to life imprisonment, baby, and I'll be
the warden.

ANGELA

You're mad.

SOL

We're a famous couple, Angela. We're gonna stay that, in public if
not in private.

ANGELA

And this will bring you happiness?

SOL

Nobody makes a dirty joke out of Sol P. Sussman. You're my
possession. I own you the same as I own every toilet in this house.

Sol feels a sudden pain in his stomach.

ANGELA

Sol, are you all right?

SOL

Don't get your hopes up. It's not a heart attack. Just this damn
constipation. I haven't taken a decent crap since I landed in
Madrid.

Sol starts for the door.

SOL (CONT'D)

Oh, and Angela, if you think you'll forget your troubles by
indulging in a shopping spree, think again. I'm canceling all of
your charge cards. From now on, all requests come through the
warden's office.

Sol leaves the room. Angela sits at her dressing table. Utterly trapped,
she gazes at her reflection in the mirror. A smaller magnifying mirror
also reflects her image.

We see, in fact, two faces of Angela, both desperate.

INT. ANGELA'S BEDROOM – NIGHT

Angela lies awake in the dark, her face white with anxiety. She lights a
cigarette, then, rises from her bed and throws on her robe.

INT. THE UPSTAIRS HALLWAY – NIGHT

Angela moves stealthily through the dark hallway, trying not to wake anyone.

EXT. THE POTTING SHED – NIGHT

Angela crosses the lawn, and after checking to see if she's been watched, enters her small potting shed. A small light is turned on but then the shade is quickly drawn.

INT. THE POTTING SHED – NIGHT

The small, rough-hewn shed is filled with the paraphernalia required by a first-rate horticulturist. Angela nearly knocks over a small earthenware pot but catches it just in time. She crosses to a small cabinet filled with bottles containing plant foods and insecticides. One small vial intrigues Angela. On the label is a skull and crossbones. She twists open the top and smells its contents. She tucks the tiny vial into her cleavage and exits the shed.

INT. THE SUSSMAN KITCHEN – NIGHT

Angela reenters the house through the kitchen door. She crosses to the living room.

INT. THE SUSSMAN LIVING ROOM – NIGHT

She gingerly heads toward the stairs. She's suddenly blinded by the harsh glare of a flashlight. It's Angela's good-looking twenty-year-old son, LANCE. He shines the flashlight under his chin, making him look like someone out of a horror film.

                    ANGELA
Lance! You scared the bejesus out of me.

Angela switches on a light.

                    LANCE
Kiss me, you beautiful creature.

She gives him a peck on the lips.

                    ANGELA
Do I smell pot?

                    LANCE
Gee, Mom, you got me on that one.

                    ANGELA
Listen, baby. I'm not one of your friends' square old ladies. I

toured with a band. I'm quite familiar with reefer. And fully acquainted with its dangers.

                                    LANCE
You're the coolest mom ever.

                                   ANGELA
What are you doing home from school?

                                    LANCE
The anti-war demonstration. The students took over the president's office. They sent the rest of us kids home.

                                   ANGELA
                                (skeptically)
Oh, really.

                                    LANCE
My friend Ruth gave the associate dean a saltwater enema.

                                   ANGELA
I need a drink.

INT. THE DEN — NIGHT

Angela and Lance have adjoined to the den; a large room with sofas, an entertainment center, and bar. The walls are covered with framed photos of Angela with the likes of Ethel Merman, Ernie Kovacs, and President Eisenhower, as well as her *Life, Look,* and *TV Guide* magazine covers.

Angela pours drinks at the bar.

                                   ANGELA
Scotch for me. Pepsi for you.

                                    LANCE
Oh, Mom.

                                   ANGELA
Well, I suppose a splash of bourbon won't kill you.

She pours a bit of whiskey in his drink.

                             ANGELA (CONT'D)
Darling, turn off that ghastly overhead and flick on the lamp.

Lance switches off the light. He turns on the lamp and compulsively begins switching it on and off over and over.

ANGELA (CONT'D)

Lance, stop it. Please.

With great effort, he leaves the lamp on. The room's suffused with a
warm glow. Lance joins her on the sofa. He falls into a deep funk.
Angela tries to break his strange mood by swinging her legs onto
Lance's lap and pulling up her nightgown to just above her knees. Her
action is not as perverse as it may seem. It's more a sadly sweet
attempt to experience an innocent teenage life she never knew.

ANGELA (CONT'D)

Be honest. Have you ever seen such gorgeous gams?

LANCE

Hmmm, well maybe on the homecoming queen.

Angela playfully pushes him down on the sofa for that remark. He's
not in the mood to roughhouse.

LANCE (CONT'D)

Mother, I told you a lie. I didn't come home because of an anti-
war demonstration. They kicked my ass out of that college. The
bastards. They said I was a bad influence.

ANGELA

On the other students?

LANCE

On the faculty. They said I was a sexual magnet.

ANGELA

I imagine it was some predatory older woman.

LANCE

Doctor Crenshaw is a man.

ANGELA

You were alone with him?

LANCE

Not alone. There were eight of them. The entire math department,
in fact. The dean said, well he said I instigated a homosexual orgy
in the faculty lounge. They found me being spun around nude on
the lazy Susan.

ANGELA

Just tell me this, the truth, and I'll be behind you, one hundred per
cent, no matter what you say. Are you – are you a cocksucker?

LANCE

Oh, Mother, who the Hell cares? I'm a mental cripple. A cripple!

ANGELA

Don't ever say that!

LANCE

I'm different. I've always been different, since I was born. I'm sick!
Twisted! A freak!

ANGELA

That's not true. And you have two parents who adore you.

LANCE

You know my father hates me. And he hates you too. Why can't
he just die?

Lance runs out of the room. Angela is suddenly aware of the vial of
arsenic hidden near her breast. Her plans are becoming firmer.

EXT. THE SUSSMAN HOME – DAY

An exterior of the Sussman home, the following day.

INT. HALLWAY – DAY

Bootsie is carrying a large basket full of laundry. Bootsie is disturbed
by the loud acid rock music emanating from Lance's room. She peers
into his open doorway and finds Lance in the act of painting on the
wall two identical twin nude male figures with enormous erections.
Bootsie shakes her head in dismay and moves on.

As she passes by the closed door to Sol's office, she hears his agonized
voice on the phone. She puts her ear to the door.

INT. SOL'S OFFICE – DAY

An anguished Sol is talking on the phone.

SOL

Monday? That's impossible. You gotta give me . . . You gotta . . .
Please.

INT. THE HALLWAY OUTSIDE SOL'S DEN – DAY

Bootsie hears Sol hang up and moan "My God . . . My God!" She
opens the door and sees Sol with his head in his hands. She comes
inside the office.

INT. SOL'S DEN – DAY

Bootsie sits in the chair opposite Sol's desk.

> BOOTSIE
>
> Mr. S, are you sick? Should I call Doctor Mandel?

> SOL
>
> Nathan Mandel I don't need.

> BOOTSIE
>
> Talk to Bootsie. Let her help.

> SOL
>
> I'm out of date. Out of touch. My kind of films, pleas for tolerance
> for the Jew, the Negro, the immigrant Italian, are made a mockery
> of today. These kids with the beards seek to tear down the
> establishment. When the fuck did I become the establishment?

> BOOTSIE
>
> You're a great man, Mr. S.

> SOL
>
> I'm finished. Kaput. It's Angela. She's a witch. She put the curse on
> me.

> BOOTSIE
>
> He that is slow to anger is better than the mighty. Proverbs, 16.

> SOL
>
> You're right. She's not worth it. Bootsie, the only way I could
> finance this new picture was to borrow money from . . . less than
> reputable associates.

> BOOTSIE
>
> The mob?

> SOL
>
> The Gods have turned against me. The rotten weather. Actors
> dying. Now the picture's fallen apart and these – associates are
> threatening to bathe me in cement if I don't pay up. Bootsie,
> you're looking at a corpse.

Sol begins to cry. Bootsie goes to his side of the desk and pushes his
head to her breast to comfort him. The expression on her face goes
from pleasure at their new intimacy, to sadness at his situation, to a
steely resolve to save him.

EXT. THE SWIMMING POOL – DAY

Angela enjoys a leisurely afternoon swim.

INT. ANGELA'S BEDROOM – DAY

Bootsie lifts Angela's lingerie out of the laundry basket and places it in the top drawer of the bureau. Her hand stumbles across the vial of arsenic. Intrigued, she unscrews the cap and puts the tiniest bit on her tongue. She violently gags and spits it out. It's clearly poison. She hears splashing in the pool outside. She looks out the window and over her shoulder, Angela is seen swimming laps.

EXT. THE SWIMMING POOL – DAY

Angela steps out of the pool. Still shapely in her white bathing suit, she throws on a glamorous flowing robe.

INT. ANGELA'S BEDROOM – DAY

Bootsie watches Angela leave the pool area. She takes another long look at the vial in her hand and ponders what further action to take.

INT. THE DINING ROOM – NIGHT

The Sussman family is dining at home. They are in the midst of the first course: soup. Sol is at the head of the table, glowering menacingly at Angela, who is seated at the opposite end. Edie sits beside him, gazing adoringly. Lance is next to Angela. Lance's compulsive behavior is manifesting itself in the way he takes a spoonful of soup, blows on it, and then puts it back. He repeats the same action over and over.

> ANGELA
> It's a damn pity you kids aren't interested in going with us to the theater tonight. *The House of Atreus* may have been written over a thousand years ago, but the murder of King Agamemnon by his Queen, Clytemnestra, is remarkably relevant to our contemporary anxieties.

Sol can't take any more of Lance's compulsive behavior.

> SOL
> Lance, just drink the goddamn soup!

> LANCE
> Sorry, Daddy.

Lance cowers. Angela tries to comfort him. Angela and Lance begin to speak in their secret language, which is translated in subtitles.

> ANGELA
> Bi con't dlame ou. Fa goup hinks. (I don't blame you. The soup stinks.)

LANCE
Hit jells gike lirty mocks. (It smells like dirty socks.)

Closeup of Edith, steaming that she's left out of their secret language.

ANGELA
Ootsie vuts wour zad's zup yand ows em bin ca doup. (Bootsie cuts your dad's up and throws them in the soup.)

This last remark cracks Lance up. He spits up the soup and that makes him laugh even louder. Sol throws down his napkin, rises from the table, and grabs Lance by the collar, yanking the boy out of his seat.

SOL
If you can't eat normal, we're gonna shut you away in an institution!

LANCE
No, Daddy, don't!

ANGELA
How dare you talk to your son like that?

SOL
It's my shame to have borne such a son.

ANGELA
The great man. The conscience of the industry. How about some tolerance and sympathy for your own family?

SOL
I've got no sympathy for you, baby. Or him. My son, the loser!

LANCE
You're the loser! The flop!

Sol belts him across the face. Lance is stunned.

ANGELA
Lance!

Lance runs out of the room. We hear him leave the house, slamming the front door. The noise upsets the dogs, who we hear barking offscreen.

SOL
Little monsters. They get put to sleep tomorrow.

Bootsie enters carrying the tray of roast beef.

SOL (CONT'D)
Angela, sit down. Sit down!

Angela takes her place at the end of the table. While Bootsie serves the main course, Angela stares malevolently at Sol. A lioness protecting her cub and a woman desperate for a last chance at happiness, she knows what she must do.

INT. A LIMOUSINE, DRIVING – NIGHT

Angela and Sol are seated in the back of a limousine on their way back from the theater. Angela is flipping through her playbill.

ANGELA
The murder scene was beautifully staged. It made the character of Clytemnestra almost sympathetic. Aren't you glad I made you renew our theater subscription?

SOL
Shut up. The best performance tonight was you pretending to be a wife.

Angela glares at Sol from her corner of the limousine. She fantasizes that she's Queen Clytemnestra in Ancient Greece.

INT. THE ROYAL BEDCHAMBER – ANCIENT GREECE – NIGHT

A highly stylized darkened palace bedchamber. King Agamemnon (Sol) is lolling in his bath. Clytemnestra (Angela) appears from behind a drape, dagger in her hand. Stealthily, she approaches the king and with demonic force, plunges the dagger into his breast.

INT. A LIMOUSINE, DRIVING – NIGHT

Angela awakes from her reverie and continues to stare at Sol with murder in her eyes.

EXT. THE SUSSMAN HOME – NIGHT

Sol's bedroom light is on.

INT. SOL'S BEDROOM – NIGHT

Sol is lying in his bed reading *Variety*. Edith opens the door and enters, wearing her nightgown.

EDITH
Daddy, I saw the light on under your door. It's after two in the morning. Are you okay?

                              SOL
Of course, my precious. I just had trouble sleeping.

                             EDITH
Are you and Mother not speaking?

                              SOL
Everything's fine. She's in the kitchen right now fixing me some
warm milk.

INT. THE SUSSMAN KITCHEN – NIGHT

Angela pours milk into a pan. She turns on a burner and heats up the
milk. Her heart is pounding. She's about to murder her husband and
can't afford to make any mistakes.

INT. SOL'S BEDROOM – NIGHT

Edith cuddles with her father on the bed.

                             EDITH
You've seemed so sad and tired ever since you got back from
Spain. What's wrong, Daddy? You can tell me. We're soul mates.

                              SOL
Then I'll confide in you. It's this God-awful constipation. Before I
go to sleep, I'm supposed to take a suppository. Nobody said it
was going to be easy being an old Jew.

INT. THE SUSSMAN KITCHEN – NIGHT

Angela takes the milk from the stove and carefully pours it into a mug.
She removes the vial of poison out of her cleavage. She is about to
drop some of the arsenic into the milk when a hand touches her
shoulder. Startled, she spins around, spilling some of the milk on her
nightgown. She screams. It's Bootsie standing behind her.

                            ANGELA
Bootsie! Don't ever do that!

                            BOOTSIE
I'm sorry, Mrs. S. I heard someone down here and I got scared.

                            ANGELA
Well, you scared the Hell out of me. Now, you – go back to bed.

                            BOOTSIE
Is that warm milk for Mr. S? I'll fix it for him.

DIE, MOMMIE, DIE   119

ANGELA

No, you won't.

BOOTSIE

Some honey and a dash of cinnamon makes it special.

ANGELA

I'll do that, dear. Now scoot.

BOOTSIE

Don't let it curdle.

ANGELA

You heard me. Scoot.

Bootsie, suspicious, begrudgingly leaves the room. Angela gingerly pours some of the arsenic into the milk and stirs.

INT. SOL'S BEDROOM – NIGHT

Edith lies in her father's arms.

SOL

Never forget that you're half Sussman. The other half, the strange Canadian goyishe flotsam, that you can dismiss.

EDITH

It's your blood that I'm proud of.

SOL

My daughter, you are my immortality. What is our motto?

EDITH

"Make it big. Give it class. Leave 'em with a message."

Angela enters carrying the mug of hot milk.

ANGELA

My, we have a visitor.

EDITH

I'll be leaving.

ANGELA

I. Magnin is having a sale on Go Go boots. We could make a day of it.

EDITH

Go Go boots? They're as ancient as a hoop skirt.

ANGELA

Then I could use your able assistance as fashion consultant.

EDITH

My first advice, Mother, would be to cancel your next facelift and start acting your age. Good night, Daddy. Pleasant dreams.

Edith kisses Sol and climbs out of the bed.

ANGELA

A kiss?

Edith gives her a chilly peck on the cheek and leaves.

ANGELA (CONT'D)

You two must have had quite an interesting little chat.

SOL

I didn't have to tell her anything new to make her despise you.

ANGELA

Drink your milk before it gets cold.

Sol picks up the mug but stops before it reaches his lips. Angela nearly winces from the suspense.

SOL

Oh, by the way, an envelope arrived for you today. The contract from Kutshers resort. Turned out you weren't lying about that singing engagement in the Catskills.

ANGELA

You opened my mail?

SOL

I phoned them today, acting as your agent. Regretfully, they couldn't meet our requests and were forced to cancel the gig. Sorry, dear, just trying to help.

Angela, enraged by this latest act of cruelty, does her best to control her emotions.

ANGELA

You do seem to be holding all the cards. Aren't you going to drink your milk?

SOL

I hate warm milk. Take it away.

ANGELA

Is it because I suggested it?

SOL

I hate warm milk. Makes me gag.

ANGELA

It will help you sleep.

SOL

I can't sleep because of the constipation. What I've gotta do is take this friggin' suppository.

He takes a huge wrapped suppository out of a box on his nightstand.

SOL (CONT'D)

How are you supposed to open this damn thing? I've got no nails.

ANGELA

Let me do it.

She takes the suppository and has a sudden realization that she can kill him by dipping the suppository into the poisoned milk. With trembling fingers, she immerses it in the mug.

SOL

Angela, Angela, what time has wrought. I remember when I first laid eyes on you in that forcockta recording studio on Fifty-third Street. So lovely and fresh.

While soaking the suppository in the poisoned milk, Angela, too, is awash in bittersweet nostalgia for what might have been, the lost chances, the tragically missed connections. For a moment, she hesitates in her resolve to carry out her drastic plan.

SOL (CONT'D)
(in his own world)

And I said to myself "Someday that delicate songbird's gonna be mine and I'm gonna boff her brains out."

Sol's vulgar interpretation of the past reinforces her decision not to turn back.

ANGELA

Here we are. Ready for insertion.

SOL

How the Hell am I gonna get this huge thing in? Throw it out and I'll drink some Milk of Magnesia.

ANGELA

You know that never works or the Ex-Lax.

SOL

Maybe after a good night's sleep, my natural peristaltic action will kick in.

ANGELA

You spent the money. You might as well try it.

SOL

It's the size of a Nathan's hotdog. I can't do this.

ANGELA
(Desperately)

I'll help you.

She takes the suppository from him.

SOL

Are you kidding?

ANGELA

I'm tired of hearing you complain about the bloat. Now, bend over. Come on, Sol. Bend over.

Camera moves away from them and through an arch and pans over a wall of framed photos of the couple in far happier days. Their voices are heard from the next room.

SOL (O.S.)

Just be careful. I've got a hemorrhoid. I can't believe this. Ow! You're killing me.

ANGELA (O.S.)

Now you know how I felt every night you forced yourself on me.

SOL (O.S.)

Ow! Motherfucker!!

ANGELA (O.S.)

I'm just trying to get the whole thing in. You're very tight. You must do your utmost to relax.

SOL (O.S.)

Relax? With a nuclear warhead up my rectum?

Camera returns to the bedroom. Sol sits painfully on the bed. Angela, in shock by what she's just done, finds it difficult to look at him.

ANGELA

Operation complete.

SOL

I wonder how long it takes before I feel anything.

ANGELA

Almost immediately from what I understand.

SOL

You've got a queer expression on your face. What are you thinking?

ANGELA

Perhaps how nothing turns out exactly as one plans.

SOL

Lady, that goes double. How many millions did I sink into that cinematic musical abortion for you to star in, *The Song of Marie Antoinette*? Every critic coast to coast agreed that overnight you'd lost your talent. That flop marked the beginning of my downfall.

Sol's venomous words jolt Angela out of her paralyzing guilt and restore some of her anger and strength. Sol gradually feels the poison taking effect.

SOL (CONT'D)

Oy, my insides are churning. I guess it's kicking in.

ANGELA

When I was young and so in love with you, I never thought it would end this way.

SOL

End? What do you mean? The suppository? Poisoned? You poisoned it, didn't you? Angela, please, for the love of God, call a para-medic. Please.

Sol staggers out of the chair and crawls toward her. He grabs hold of her nightgown. Aghast, she pushes him away. He attempts to crawl to the telephone. Angela is frozen.

Sol tries to reach for the telephone but collapses on the floor. He writhes in agony.

SOL (CONT'D)

Angela, Angela! Rot in Hell!

Sol lies there, dead. Angela's immediate desire is to flee from the horror. At the last moment, she notices the mug, picks it up, and runs into the adjoining bathroom.

EXT. BEDROOM BALCONY – NIGHT

Angela comes out onto the balcony and tries to catch her breath. Barely composed, she opens the bedroom door and SCREAMS.

ANGELA
Oh my God, someone come in here quick. Lance! Bootsie! Edith!

INT. THE LIVING ROOM – NIGHT

TWO ORDERLIES are carrying Sol out of the house in a body bag. The flashing lights from the police car and ambulance outside add to the hysteria of the moment. Bootsie is clearly in charge. Edith is sobbing. Angela, clutching one of the dogs, places her other arm around her daughter but Edith pushes her away. Lance cowers by the stairs. A handsome POLICEMAN taking notes on a pad continues questioning Angela.

POLICEMAN
Mrs. Sussman, was your husband on any heart medications?

ANGELA
Dozens. I pooh poohed his aches and pains, called him a pathetic, neurotic hypochondriac. I'll live forever with the guilt.

LANCE
Mom, it's not your fault. Pop had a bum ticker.

POLICEMAN
Were you in charge of your husband's medications?

Bootsie crosses to them and takes Angela's arm.

BOOTSIE
No more questions. Can't you see the poor dear is in a total state of shock? Mrs. S, you go back on upstairs.

ANGELA
I'm his wife. I'm going in the ambulance with him. You can't stop me!

EDITH
Mother, must you always be acting!

BOOTSIE

Mrs. S, it's best that I go. You're much too fragile and way too famous.

POLICEMAN

Mrs. Sussman, that'll be all for now. You've been very helpful.

ANGELA

And you're a delight. I can't get over it. All of you are so darned good looking. You could be actors.

EXT. THE SWIMMING POOL AND PATIO – DAY

The following day. Edith is seated by the edge of the pool, wracked with sobs. Tony enters from the house.

EDITH

How dare you show your face in this house, less than twenty-four hours after my father's death?

TONY

I'm sorry you feel that way, Edith. But perhaps I can be of some comfort to your mother.

EDITH

Well, I'm afraid you can't. Mother is out with my brother, Lance. He's helping her adjust to her new widowhood.

EXT. A STREET IN BEVERLY HILLS – DAY

A street lined with beautiful homes. We hear the ROAR of a motorcycle. From around the corner comes Lance racing by on his Harley. Holding tightly around his waist is Angela, garbed in tight black pants, a black windbreaker, and a matching black helmet. They both laugh and scream against the wind.

EXT. THE SWIMMING POOL AND PATIO – DAY

Edith kicks the water violently and looks up at Tony.

EDITH

What kind of crazy world is this? My father's dead and my mother's gigolo shows up ready for some hot action.

TONY

I suppose I deserve that. Would you believe that the last thing I wanted to do was betray your father?

EDITH

Yeah, like really.

TONY

I don't ask for your forgiveness. But it was almost as if I had no choice. Your mother is a sorceress. She casts a hypnotic spell over a man. You possess that same magic, Edith.

EDITH
(vulnerably)
I do? No. You're not to be trusted.

EXT. THE SWIMMING POOL – DAY

LATER

Tony's charms have been most persuasive. He and Edith are now having sex in the pool. Tony probes deeper.

TONY

Edie, lovely, smooth, sweet Edie, I want to know everything about you. Your favorite color, your favorite movie star. Do you think your mother killed your father?

EDITH

Canary yellow, Carol Lynley, and yes, I know she did it. But I can't prove a thing. Tony, I think you just broke my hymen.

EXT. THE SWIMMING POOL AND PATIO – DAY

LATER

Edith and Tony, wearing towels, are now having a post-coital cigarette on two recliners on the patio.

TONY

I told you there wouldn't be much blood and you see, the chlorine dissolved it. Where were we? I heard your father died of a massive heart attack.

EDITH

So they said. But there's something not right about it.

TONY

As a man of the world, I have friends in interesting places. Allow me to do a little leg work?

EDITH

Yeah. Sure. But I thought you were under my mother's spell?

TONY

Haven't you heard? There's a new witch in town.

EXT. THE OUTSIDE OF THE SUSSMAN HOUSE – DAY

The following day. Angela, followed by Bootsie, exits the house through the front door. They are both dressed in black mourning. They wait outside for Edith.

ANGELA
Where is Edith? We're going to be late for the funeral.

BOOTSIE
I do worry about that child. But as my wise Uncle Enoch used to say, "What catsup is to meatloaf, so sorrow is a condiment to joy."

Edith, in the heaviest widow's weeds, leaves the house.

EDITH
I'm ready to kill Lance. He's locked himself in his room.

ANGELA
He's not going.

EDITH
Not going to Daddy's funeral? He's going, if I have to break down that door.

ANGELA
Don't you say a word to him. Lance is taking it very hard. I've never seen the lad so "distrait."

EXT. THE BACK OF THE SUSSMAN HOUSE – DAY

LATER

A short while later, Lance is dancing around the backyard, nude and strumming his guitar. Tony walks up and approaches him.

TONY
Nice breeze. Must feel good.

LANCE
What are you doing on my lawn?

TONY
The name's Tony Parker. You . . . you must be Lance. I'm here to offer my condolences to your mother. Isn't she back from the funeral?

LANCE
After the service, there was a reception at Peter Lawford's agents.

TONY

May I ask why you're not with the rest of your family?

LANCE

That's none of your business.

Carefully holding the guitar over his crotch, Lance runs past the side of the house. Tony follows him.

Lance, conflicted about his feelings for Tony, dashes into the potting shed and shuts the door.

INT. THE POTTING SHED – DAY

CONTINUOUS

Lance, still nude, cowers in the corner. Tony slowly opens the door and lets himself in.

He lights up a cigarette. Lance is fascinated.

TONY

You know, I skipped out on my old man's funeral. Ghastly primitive ritual.

LANCE

I don't like sad things.

TONY

We've met before, a long time ago. At the Hacienda Club. Your father brought you around. I remember you in the locker room, a scrawny waif with no pubic hair.

LANCE

I remember you too. You didn't wear a towel.

TONY

No need to be shy around men. Still collect photos of Donald O'Connor?

LANCE

Yeah.

Tony sits down on a stool.

TONY

Wonderful lady, your mother. I understand she was very kind to her sister, your Aunt Barbara.

LANCE

Why not? They were close.

TONY

Were they? How much do you remember?

LANCE

Why do you want to know?

TONY

I'm sorry. I suppose I'm just nosy. Terrible habit. I find people so fascinating. You intrigue me very much.

LANCE

Why?

TONY

Because you dare to be yourself. Honesty. It's a big turn-on to me. A real big turn-on.

Tony moves over to where Lance is seated. Lance is transfixed by his crotch.

TONY (CONT'D)

You remember it from the locker room. You want it, don't you?

LANCE

Uh huh.

Lance reaches for Tony's zipper. Tony pushes his hand away.

TONY

Only after you've answered my questions. Tell me about your mother and Aunt Barbara.

LANCE

You can't bully me. My family is very private.

TONY

Perhaps I'll speak to your mother some other time.
Lance grabs Tony's belt.

LANCE

Buster, if you want any singing out of me, you better haul out that bratwurst and spread some mustard on it.

TONY

A deal's a deal.

Lance gets on his knees in front of Tony and starts to unzip him.

INT. PETER LAWFORD'S LIVING ROOM – DAY

THE SCREENPLAYS OF CHARLES BUSCH

A large Hollywood-style living room decorated in the height of Sixties Rich Hip. The room is filled with the elite of the movie business. Angela is seated on the sofa surrounded by men. Edith sits sullenly in the corner, her "duenna" Bootsie standing protectively beside her. WAITERS carrying trays of hors d'oeuvres and martinis scoot around.

A dignified man in his sixties, the producer, SAM FISHBEIN, stands by the fireplace and addresses the room.

> FISHBEIN
> Let us mourn the loss of a warrior king. Felled not on the field of battle but by coronary thrombosis.

Angela flags down a waiter carrying drinks and takes one.

> FISHBEIN (CONT'D)
> As a producer myself, I would have preferred to see a man of Sol Sussman's stature lying in state, a draped catafalque, burning tapers. I am distressed that such a man should be hurriedly cremated like a mongrel dog at the pound.

Bootsie and Edith look at each other meaningfully.

> BOOTSIE
> Amen. The truth at last is spoken.

Angela sips her drink with an air of cool nonchalance.

While Fishbein continues his eulogy, SHATZI VAN ALLEN, a well-known female gossip columnist, sits beside Angela on the sofa. She whispers conspiratorially to Angela.

> SHATZI
> Where was this schmuck when Sol's picture flushed down that Spanish crapper? How are you bearing up, Sweetie? You look, of course, divine. Is that a Givenchy on your back?

> ANGELA
> Shatzi, is this for publication?

> SHATZI
> Doesn't have to be. You do consider me a friend?

> ANGELA
> Always. And that's definitely for publication.

> SHATZI
> I doubt you'd get a record deal anywhere but there's still television.

Let's just say that I'm working on the voice. It's been a long time between songs.

SHATZI

There's a piano. Why don't you give us all a thrill?

ANGELA

It's hardly appropriate.

A waiter passes by again with a tray of martinis. Angela hands him her empty glass and takes another cocktail.

INT. PETER LAWFORD'S LIVING ROOM – DAY

LATER

A short time later and Angela is nestled beside the piano player, drink in hand, wailing the opening phrase of the gospel song "Sometimes I Feel Like A Motherless Child."

Edith, livid, glares at her from across the room.

INT. PETER LAWFORD'S LIVING ROOM – DAY

LATER

A short time after that, Angela is warmed up and wowing the crowd with a frenetic jazz arrangement of "Won't You Come Home, Bill Bailey." There are now three empty martini glasses sitting on the piano.

INT. PETER LAWFORD'S LIVING ROOM – DAY

LATER

A short time after that, Angela has really let loose. There are now four empty martini glasses sitting on the piano. Angela is frugging wildly with two sexy LOUNGE LIZARDS. She's gone very contemporary and is belting out "Spinning Wheel."

Edith turns away from this spectacle in revulsion.

INT. THE SUSSMAN LIVING ROOM – NIGHT

The front door opens and Edith and Bootsie enter.

EDITH

I always knew Mother was nothing more than a cheap, hopped up nymphomaniac.

Lance comes downstairs, still buttoning his fly. Tony follows him.

> LANCE
> Wow, you weren't gone very long.

> EDITH
> Tony, what are you doing here?

> TONY
> Your brother was kind enough to show me his fresco. Quite impressive for a boy his age.

> EDITH
> Lance, how could you miss the funeral?

> LANCE
> Stop browbeating me. I'm very upset.

> BOOTSIE
> Sometimes you have to face things that are hard to swallow.

Lance gazes wistfully at Tony's crotch.

Angela enters through the front door.

> ANGELA
> All in all, I think it was a lovely service and reception. Hello, Tony. How kind of you to join us in our mourning.

> TONY
> Nothing could keep me away.

> ANGELA
> Bootsie, remove some of these floral tributes. They're wilting and I can't bear to be surrounded by more death.

Bootsie lifts a vase of flowers.

> BOOTSIE
> I think I'll press some of these petals in the pages of my bible.

> ANGELA
> As you wish.

Bootsie exits into the kitchen.

> TONY
> I have a small gift for you. Something to cheer you up.

ANGELA

You have a gift for thoughtfulness. What is it?

Tony walks to the stereo and starts the 78 player.

TONY

The one record you and your sister made when you were a singing duo. "The Salt and Pepper Polka."

The music of the record triggers a violent response from Angela. She immediately smashes the record.

ANGELA

How dare you bring that monstrosity into this house?

TONY

But it was the only recording of you and Barbara ever released.

LANCE

The only existing record of her voice.

ANGELA

And I will not be reminded of her by anyone!

TONY

I didn't mean to upset you.

ANGELA
(in volcanic rage)

You knew perfectly well that I hate listening to my old records, yet you deliberately shoved it under my nose. And always the questions, the snooping about. Well, I will not be tortured and tormented.

TONY

But Angela –

ANGELA

I want you out of my life! I want you out of my house! Just get out!

TONY

You can't discard me like one of your false eyelashes. This is Tony. I'm in for the long haul.

ANGELA

Out!

TONY

You and I made some heavy promises, baby!

ANGELA

Get out!

TONY

You haven't heard the last of me!

Tony exits through the front door. Angela slams it shut.

ANGELA

And that goes for all of you. I'm clearing out the dead wood. This is as good a time as any to announce that I'm selling the house to the first bidder.

EDITH

You wouldn't!

ANGELA

I'm moving to New York. Edith, I don't want to hear a word about it. I am sick and tired of living my life for others. This is the time for Angela Arden. This time it's for me! For me! For me!

She pours herself a drink.

ANGELA (CONT'D)

I hate this house. I hate these walls. I hate this sofa! The only part of this dump that doesn't make me puke is that door because that's the way I'm getting out!

Like a caged panther, she strides around the room.

ANGELA (CONT'D)

I'm bringing down these walls around us. To quote the kids in the ghetto, "Burn, baby, Burn"!

She hurls her glass of scotch into the fireplace. The alcohol explodes into a terrifying ball of flame.

INT. A COFFEE SHOP – DAY

Lance and Edith are seated in a booth at a coffee shop.

LANCE

Edie, aren't you gonna eat your cole slaw?

EDITH

It's time you faced the truth. Our mother murdered our father.

                    LANCE
Hold the cole slaw.

                    EDITH
She poisoned him.

                    LANCE
He died of a heart attack.

                    EDITH
Many rich old men who die of heart attacks were really the
victims of arsenic poisoning.

                    LANCE
But Bootsie told us she was with the coroner when he performed
the autopsy. There wasn't a trace of arsenic in his stomach.

                    EDITH
But what if Mother was clever and found another way to slip him
the arsenic. A method devised to bypass the digestive tract.

                    LANCE
I'm confused.

                    EDITH
The night Daddy died, he was complaining of constipation. A
doctor prescribed a powerful suppository. Suppose Mother found
a way of tampering with the laxative.

                    LANCE
I don't believe it.

                    EDITH
You're Sol Sussman's only son. It's up to you to avenge his death.

                    LANCE
I couldn't.

                    EDITH
I'll stand by you. I know I haven't always been a good sister. I've
teased you, shaved your head, tried to blind you. But I was young
and immature. I've done a lot of growing up in the last forty-eight
hours.

                    LANCE
What do you want me to do?

                    EDITH
Kill mother.

LANCE

No!

CUT TO

EXT. OUTSIDE THE SUSSMAN HOUSE – DAY

A moving van pulls up to the house. Two good-looking young
MOVING MEN get out and ring the bell. Angela opens the door.

MOVING MAN
We're here for the furniture. How many rooms it gonna be?

ANGELA
Just one. My late husband's office. This way, gentlemen.

She leads the men inside and closes the door.

CUT TO

INT. OUTSIDE THE COFFEE SHOP'S MEN'S ROOM – DAY

Lance runs inside the men's room. Edith shouts to him just as a man
exits.

EDITH
Why can't you accept that Mother is a murderess and a whore!

Edith charges into the men's room.

INT. THE COFFEE SHOP MEN'S ROOM – DAY

Edith sees three stalls. She moves toward the stall in the corner.

EDITH
Lance, you can't hide from me or the truth. Lance!

LANCE
(from inside the booth)
Leave me alone! I'm not listening to you.

Edith climbs onto the sink and leans over the stall, looking down on
Lance.

EDITH
You will listen.

LANCE
Leave me alone! My head, it's pounding! Pounding!

Yes, it's pounding. Sometimes it feels like you've got an atom bomb inside your skull that's ready to go "pow"!

LANCE

Get out of here!

EDITH

It's time you heard the truth. Daddy told me it was the drugs, the pill popping Mother did during her pregnancy that made you the way you are.

LANCE

Leave me alone!

Lance gets up from the toilet and leaves the stall.

Lance goes to the sink. He splashes water on his face. Edith leans against the men's room door.

EDITH

There was something wrong with your brain. Made you a little slow. Made it hard for you to understand things.

LANCE

What?

EDITH

But don't you see? It's not your fault. It's hers. Because Mother was so selfish and evil that she wouldn't give up her precious sleeping pills.

A man exits a stall and moves over to the sink. Edith glares at him.

EDITH (CONT'D)

Fuck off!! Lance, she destroyed you! She turned your brains into mush! Into creamed spinach!

LANCE

She didn't! It's not true! You're the bitch. You're the one I'd like to kill!

Lance runs out of the men's room. Edith, breathless, gives up.

EXT. A SUBURBAN ROAD – DAY

Lance, hysterical, is riding home on his motorcycle. A close-up of his anguished, tear-stained face.

LANCE (V.O.)
She couldn't do such a thing. She couldn't. Not Mother.

EXT. OUTSIDE THE SUSSMAN HOUSE – DAY

Lance pulls up in the driveway. He sees the moving van and is very confused at seeing his father's office furniture standing outside on the gravel. He enters the house.

INT. THE LIVING ROOM – DAY

Lance looks around for his mother.

LANCE
Mother? Mother?

Lance decides to look for Angela upstairs.

INT. THE UPSTAIRS HALL – DAY

Lance thinks he hears something from behind Angela's closed door.

LANCE
Mother?

Lance opens her door and gets quite an eyeful.

INT. ANGELA'S BEDROOM – DAY

CONTINUOUS

Angela, on the bed with just a sheet wrapped around her, is in the midst of a three-way with the two nude moving men. One is standing on the bed and it appears that the lady of the house is going down on him and the other seems to be mounting his hostess from the rear.

Angela, startled, looks up. Her first irrational reaction is to scream.

ANGELA
What are you doing in here? Get out! Get out!

LANCE
Oh, my God!

Lance runs out of the room and we can hear him GALLOP down the stairs and out of the house. Angela is suddenly filled with guilt and remorse. Gathering the sheet around her, she pulls away from her companions.

ANGELA
Oh, Lance. Oh, my baby.

INT. THE HALLWAY LEADING TO THE LAW OFFICE – DAY

The entrance to a very grand Beverly Hills law firm. Their name
"Melnick, Tuchman, Fein, and Glick" can be read on the door.

Edith, Lance, and Bootsie quickly stride toward the door. Angela, in
large dark sunglasses, walks several steps behind them. Edith and
Bootsie enter the law office. Angela stops Lance before he can join
them.

                    ANGELA
Lance Sussman, you are going to speak to me.

                    LANCE
Why? You're not my mother. My mother couldn't be so
disgusting.

                    ANGELA
Darling, sexual fulfillment is every woman's God-given right and
by golly, I'm going to grab it.

Lance is so revolted he can't even reply. He pushes past her and enters
the law office.

INT. A LAWYERS'S OFFICE – DAY

Sol's elegant lawyer, ELLIOTT TUCHMAN (50's), is seated behind his
impressive desk. Angela, Edith, Lance, and Bootsie sit on the sofa and
chairs in front of him.

                    TUCHMAN
Sol Sussman was not only my client but a beloved friend. Indeed,
only last Chanukah he gave me this gold desk set. I cherish the gift
as I cherished the man.

He runs his fingers along the sharp gold letter opener.

                    TUCHMAN (CONT'D)
On the morning of his death, Sol instructed me to draw up an
entirely new will. It is this new document that I feel compelled to
honor.

Angela takes out a cigarette. She turns to Lance to light it. He remains
impassive. She lights up herself.

                    TUCHMAN (CONT'D)
The children have been left substantial trusts that are protected
against any outstanding debts. Angela, I must tell you that you
have been completely cut out except for the minimal allowance
required by law.

The children gasp. Angela's face is a frozen mask.

TUCHMAN (CONT'D)
The bulk of the estate apart from the children's trusts is willed to Miss Bootsie Carp.

BOOTSIE
Blessed are the meek: for they shall inherit the earth. Matthew, 5.

ANGELA
And this will was signed?

TUCHMAN
In my presence.

ANGELA
Well. Bootsie, you were devoted and extraordinarily loyal to Mr. Sussman.

BOOTSIE
My, how that man loved my corn fritters.

ANGELA
Indeed, he did. However, I plan to contest this will. Tuchman, you better slap on your jock strap because I intend to give your cojones a mean twist. Nothing personal, Bootsie.

TUCHMAN
Mrs. Sussman, if you will excuse me for a moment. I should like to bring in my associate.

Tuchman leaves the room.

EDITH
I wonder what would make Daddy change his will. Hmmmm.

ANGELA
I am in no mood for your patented brand of bitchery, missy.

EDITH
You're not going to contest that will because if you do, there might be an investigation.

LANCE
A very thorough investigation.

BOOTSIE
Children, these walls are thin.

ANGELA

I'm changing my mind. I may not contest that will, after all. I'm going back into show business. My voice is stronger than ever. And furthermore, perhaps I'll pen my memoirs. Yes. For quite a hefty sum, I'll reveal all the dirty little details of my sham of a marriage to that late, great son of a bitch-shit-heel, Mr. Sol P. Sussman.

BOOTSIE

And destroy his good name?

EDITH

You think you can make a comeback? With your pitch problems?

Angela stands by the desk with her back to Edith.

EDITH (CONT'D)

You're nothing but a campy show biz joke. Have you forgotten your last summer stock tour of *Molly Brown*? The boos, the walk-outs, the raspberries! Unfortunately it was in the round so the management was unable to ring down the curtain! They had to drag you off the stage before the rotten eggs hit you!!

Angela loses all control, picks up the gold letter opener from off the desk, spins around, and hurls it at Edith. The letter opener sticks at a right angle out of Edith's cheek.

EDITH (CONT'D)

My face! My face!

The door to the office opens and Tuchman rushes in. The room is in a panic as everyone tries to help Edith.

EXT. OUTSIDE THE SUSSMAN HOME – DAY

Edith, Lance, and Bootsie get out of the car and walk toward the house. Angela follows behind. Edith has a small bandage criss-crossed on her cheek.

ANGELA

Dr. Ing said it was a miracle but there'd be no permanent scarring. And he was able to remove that unsightly wart from Sister's neck. So really it was all for the best –

Edith, Lance, and Bootsie enter the house, slamming the door in Angela's face.

EXT. ANGELA'S GARDEN – DAY

Later in the day, Angela is in the backyard, pruning her rose bushes. Deeply disturbed by her impulsively violent act toward Edith, she pauses for a moment. Perhaps it's the sunlight on the roses that have prompted a memory, but she is seized by an intense pang of nostalgia.

EXT. ANGELA'S GARDEN – DAY – 1954

FLASHBACK

The exact same locale thirteen years earlier. A WOMAN is lying on a chaise in the background. She's reading and so her face is obscured. EDITH and LANCE (ages 9 and 7) are playing on the ground. Angela arrives on the scene carrying gifts for the children. The children light up when they see her and rush into her arms. Their enthusiasm knocks her to the ground. She basks in their affection and romps on the lawn with them.

END OF FLASHBACK

EXT. ANGELA'S GARDEN – DAY

Angela focuses on her gardening. She looks up to find Bootsie glaring at her, the sun blazing behind her.

> BOOTSIE
> She who transgresses the laws of man shall dwell forever in the fires of Beelzebub!

> ANGELA
> That's a rather odd thing to say, Bootsie. Even from you.

> BOOTSIE
> Heathen! Purge thy sins! After twenty-five years in this house, I know all your dirty little secrets. And I mean all of 'em.

Angela rises from the flower bed and gathers her poise.

> ANGELA
> And after twenty-five years, you finally show your true colors. I must say, it's not terribly attractive.

> BOOTSIE
> Lady, I'm gonna be around your neck like an albatross till the day you leave this green earth.

Pushed, Angela drops her great lady hauteur and becomes the tough as nails Saskatchewan dame she might have been.

> ANGELA
> Listen, sister, I don't take threats from maids.

BOOTSIE

Now it's you who's showing her true colors. You never fooled me.
Not for a minute. I always knew you were nothing but trash
washed over the Canadian border.

Angela continues weeding her garden.

BOOTSIE (CONT'D)

You're never gonna write a book about Mr. Sussman because I
won't let you. You're not gonna make a penny soiling his good
name.

ANGELA

You floor-scrubbing old hag. You've got nothing on me. And even
if you did, who would believe you? You're a liar, a cheat, and a
drunk.

BOOTSIE

I dried out at one of those fancy sanitariums years ago.

ANGELA

I know how much of our booze you've been knocking back alone
in your pitiful little maid's room. You're a lonely, bitter souse,
Bootsie. And no one's gonna believe your word against mine and I
mean no one.

Angela picks up her gardening shears and basket and moves toward
the potting shed. Bootsie follows her.

BOOTSIE

Woe unto ye who makes mockery of the righteous.

Angela pauses for a moment of honest reflection. She is truly haunted
by the choices she's made in life.

ANGELA

It takes great courage to murder the first time. That's when you
can no longer claim your soul as your own.

Angela places her hands on Bootsie's shoulders. Her attitude now
changes to that of cool defiance.

ANGELA (CONT'D)

After that it becomes remarkably simple. You'd never be quite
sure what lay around the corner, would you, dear?

With sinister poise, Angela slowly walks away. Bootsie watches her
with trepidation.

INT. THE DEN – AFTERNOON

Angela enters the den, sipping a tall glass of vodka. She heads over to the piano to do her singing exercises. She plunks out a scale and begins vocalizing. Although she starts off promisingly, soon it becomes painfully clear how limited her vocal resources actually are. The truth hits her hard. Just at that moment, she looks up and sees her reflection in the mirror. The lighting is unflatteringly harsh and she stares in horror at her aging image. A wrenching cry of agony emerges from her throat and she collapses at the piano.

INT. ANGELA'S BEDROOM – DAY

Bootsie enters Angela's room. She looks around in disgust.

> BOOTSIE
> Thinks she can frighten me. Hmmph! Guess I'll just do a little laundry for her majesty.

She opens the closet, revealing a rack of beautiful gowns. She takes out a white silk gown and checks the label.

> BOOTSIE (CONT'D)
> "Dry clean only." Think we'll toss this in with Lance's new blue jeans.

She tosses the gown on the floor and pulls from the closet a black sequined gown.

> BOOTSIE (CONT'D)
> Nothing a little heavy duty Clorox won't take out.

Someone has entered the room. Bootsie looks up in great surprise.

> BOOTSIE (CONT'D)
> What? Forget something? What do you want?

From the intruder's POV, Bootsie is pushed toward the large opened window.

> BOOTSIE (CONT'D)
> Oh no, don't! Why? There's no need – please don't! Did you think I might squeal? I wouldn't. I swear. No!!!

Gloved hands grasp her neck. Bootsie struggles to get free but the intruder is too strong for her.

INT. ANGELA'S BEDROOM – DAY

Looking out into the hallway, we see Bootsie's legs pulled out of frame by the unseen intruder.

EXT. OUTSIDE THE SUSSMAN HOME – DAY

A beat up Chevy convertible pulls up. Lance is in the passenger seat. The DRIVER, a bearded, tattooed "leather daddy" pushes Lance out of the car in disgust.

> DRIVER
>
> Asshole.

The car speeds away in a dust storm of exhaust. Lance, sullenly, decides to enter the house through the side entrance. He walks toward the potting shed.

EXT. THE SIDE OF THE HOUSE – DAY

Lance gets a glimpse of Tony darting into the potting shed. Intrigued, he moves closer to the potting shed.

INT. POTTING SHED – DAY

Lance enters, catching Tony.

> LANCE
>
> What are you doing here?

> TONY
>
> I – um – was hoping to make things up with your mother.

> LANCE
>
> Why are you hiding in the potting shed?

> TONY
>
> I wasn't hiding. I merely thought it was a safe bet she'd be in here. Guess I was mistaken. Perhaps she's in the house.

Tony starts to head for the house. Lance pulls him back.

> LANCE
>
> Not so fast, sausage man. I've missed you. Missed me?

> TONY
> (uncomfortably)
>
> Yes. How have you been?

> LANCE
>
> Baby can't sleep. Needs Tony. Needs him bad.

TONY

We'll have to plan a sleepover at my pad. Perhaps next week.

LANCE

Nope. Now.

TONY

Now? Here? Are you cr –
                              (stops himself)
Are you serious?

LANCE

You were gonna say "Are you crazy?" Well, I am, baby. For you.

TONY

Lance, someone might see us.

LANCE

I guess it's tough being a switch hitter but don't worry, Tony. I'll
keep your secret. Just as long as you zig zag my way.

Lance starts to unbuckle Tony's pants. Tony tries to stop him.

TONY

Lance, your mother might come in at any second.

LANCE

Stop worrying. You'll get age lines. Tongue me.

Tony is about to kiss Lance when a drop of something red hits Lance
on the nose. Lance looks up and another drop of red hits him in the
eye.

The roof starts to creak and give way. Lance and Tony jump clear just
as the ceiling collapses and something large lands with a thud. To their
horror, they see Bootsie's body among the rubble.

INT. EDITH'S BEDROOM – NIGHT

Edith, in her nightgown, sits on her bed, reading a newspaper.

INSERT

The headline of the tabloid story reads "Arden maid a suicide," the
subtitle of the piece "New tragedy hits hard luck ex-songstress."
Accompanying the article is an old glamour photo of Angela, circa
1950.

Edith puts down the newspaper and leaves the room.

INT. THE UPSTAIRS HALLWAY – NIGHT

Edith tiptoes down the eerie, shadowy hall toward Lance's room. Angela appears at the end of the corridor, as ghostly as a phantom.

> EDITH

Mother?

Angela doesn't respond. She merely stares at her daughter.

> EDITH (CONT'D)

Mother, are you okay?

> ANGELA

Angela – Angela – why?

> EDITH

How many dolls have you taken?

Edith takes Angela by the shoulders and leads her back to her room. At the door, Angela stops and stares at her daughter with frightening intensity.

> ANGELA

Your every dream came true.

Angela retreats to her bedroom and shuts the door. Edith shudders and proceeds to her brother's room. She hears the TELEVISION behind his closed door.

INT. LANCE'S BEDROOM – NIGHT

Lance is seated on his bed, watching TV, smoking a joint, and fashioning a noose. Edith enters.

> EDITH

Lance, don't do it.

> LANCE

It's not for me, stupid. It's a Mother's Day gift.

> EDITH

Wow, when you turn, you really turn.

> LANCE

Chickening out? Can't take the heat? Huh? Huh?

> EDITH

No. But I think before we take drastic action, we should force her to confess to her crimes. I want to hear from Mother's own lips that she killed Daddy and that she killed Bootsie because Bootsie knew she killed Daddy. Or something like that.

LANCE

I had a feeling you'd require a confession of guilt. Well, what if she was under the influence of something?

EDITH

Kind of a truth serum?

LANCE

You're catching on. My plan is to send Mom on a little trip, an acid trip, LSD, a mind bender.

EDITH

LSD? Can you score some?

LANCE

Got a tab with her initials on it. Thought we'd do it tomorrow night. Put a little acid-laced sugar cube in Mother's after-dinner coffee. That'll get her talking.

INT. THE DINING ROOM – NIGHT

Angela, Lance, and Edith are seated at the dining room table. They're finishing up their dessert. Angela chatters on with vivacity, determined to get their lives on track again. Both kids pretend that they are one big happy family. She addresses Lance in their secret language. Once more, the translation appears in subtitles.

ANGELA

I'm bot cure dat to ear for ga Hoscars. Da jack Korell mor na preen Quavilla. (I'm not sure what to wear to the Oscars. The black Norell or the green Travilla.)

LANCE

Ris sa Travilla da vone with xa yinestone zim? (Is the Travilla the one with the rhinestone trim?)

ANGELA

Bon ca dollar. (On the collar.)

LANCE

Ot fa guffs? (Not the cuffs?)

ANGELA

Ni, dats ja Kanel. (No, that's the Chanel.)

EDITH

Would you two stop it? I feel so left out when you do that secret language schtick.

ANGELA

It's no secret. We've always been perfectly willing to teach you.

EDITH

Mother, let's not argue. There's been an ancient tradition of anger in this house.

ANGELA

Amen, sister. I was just asking your brother's advice on what I should wear to the Academy Awards tomorrow night. I think I'll wear my white Givenchy. White is the traditional color for mourning in India.

Edith pours coffee for herself and Lance.

EDITH

Coffee, Mother?

ANGELA

No, thank you. It'll keep me up all night.

EDITH

It's Viennese. I made it special.

ANGELA

Very well then. If it's special.

EDITH

Lance, shouldn't you get ready for the after dinner entertainment?

ANGELA

A floor show to boot. Aren't I the lucky mum?

Edith drops the LSD laced sugar cube into Angela's coffee.

INT. THE DEN – NIGHT

Angela and Edith take their coffee into the den. All the lights are out except for an illuminated area, which Lance has turned into his stage. Angela sits down on the sofa and lights up a cigarette.

ANGELA

Audience in! House lights down! Curtain up!

Lance enters in full Angela drag: wig, dress and makeup. He begins to lip-synch to one of her old records.

ANGELA (CONT'D)

How many times have I told you kids, I hate hearing my old records!

EDITH

Mother, he's worked so hard on this.

As Lance performs, Angela begins feeling the effect of the LSD. The lights appear psychedelic. Angela's recording sounds distorted and cross-fades into acid-rock music. The kids seem to be moving in slow motion.

ANGELA

What's happening? Too much bourbon.

EDITH

Mother?

ANGELA

I'm looking through the end of a kaleidoscope.

LANCE

Just turn off your mind and relax. Go with it.

Edith, surreptitiously, flicks on the switch of a reel to reel tape recorder hidden behind the sofa.

ANGELA

My body's gone. I can see right into my brain.

Angela looks up and sees above the fireplace a large poster announcing the only Saskatchewan appearance of the Arden Sisters. She hears her father's ghostly voice.

FATHER (V.O.)

I'm very proud of both of my daughters but Angela, she's the special one. She's the star.

For the rest of this acid trip sequence, for the sake of clarity, Angela will be known as BARBARA.

BARBARA

Papa? Papa?

A montage of publicity photos of the young Arden Sisters is SUPER-IMPOSED over Barbara's tormented face.

Ghostly voices from the past are heard.

THEATER OWNER #1 (V.O.)

Cincinnati's Fox Theater proudly presents those little girls with the big voices, the Arden Sisters.

The Chicago World's Fair presents those pint-size dynamos of song, The Arden Sisters.

THEATER OWNER #3(V.O.)
New York's Palace Theater presents the little crowned princesses of vaudeville, the Arden Sisters.

YOUNG ANGELA (V.O.)
Barbara, I feel awful breaking up the act. But RCA only wants me. They say you have no talent and are holding me back.

A woman's hand holding a pair of scissors cuts one of the photos in half, separating the sisters.

Close-up of Barbara today (1967).

BARBARA
But you can't leave the act, Angie. You can't!

In her mind, Barbara hears an announcer's ghostly VOICE.

ANNOUNCER (V.O.)
The newcomer of the year, star of the decade, Miss Show Business, America's nightingale, the one and only Miss Angela Arden!

Under the announcer's voiceover, we see once more the earlier clip of Angela belting out a tune on a kinescope of a 1950's television variety series.

INT. A SLEAZY NIGHTCLUB, 1948 – NIGHT

Barbara is singing the same song at a microphone in a seedy nightclub.

ANNOUNCER (V.O)
Albuquerque's Skylight Bar and Grill presents Barbara Arden, Angela Arden's sister.

While Barbara sings, some drunken customers begin pelting her with crumbled cigarette wrappers.

LADY CUSTOMER (V.O.)
She's awful. She's certainly not her sister.

INT. CBS EXECUTIVE OFFICE, 1951 – DAY

While the vocal track of Angela's triumphant song on the kinescope continues, we're now in an executive's office at CBS. Angela is seated at a desk signing a contract, surrounded by beaming executives. Behind her is a large banner reading, "CBS welcomes Angela Arden!" Cameras flash.

INT. THE GRAMMY AWARDS, 1952 — NIGHT

Angela, dripping in furs and jewels, receives her Grammy award.

> ANGELA (V.O.)
> Sister, sister, sister.

INT. A RESTAURANT, 1952 — DAY

Barbara, now a harried waitress, trips and drops an enormous tray of dishes.

> ANGELA (V.O.)
> My dear sister Barbara, a hopeless failure. My dear sister Barbara, a pathetic nobody.

INT. SUBURBAN HOUSE, 1952 — DAY

Angela's triumphant song on the kinescope continues, as we're now in the foyer of a house in the suburbs. The doorbell rings, we see the back of the lady of the house opening the front door. Standing there holding a vacuum cleaner is the door-to-door saleswoman, Barbara. Before Barbara can utter a word, the lady of the house slams the door in her face.

INT. A JEWELRY STORE, 1953 — DAY

A close-up of a beautiful jeweled necklace lying on a display table. Barbara's hand, surreptitiously, pushes the necklace into her open handbag. Suddenly, another hand, that of a store detective, grabs her arm.

INSERT

Barbara Arden's sad police mug shot.

INT. HOTEL BALLROOM, 1952 — DAY

Angela holds up her latest gold record as the cameras flash frenetically.

INT. THE GRAMMY AWARDS, 1952 — NIGHT

Angela, dripping in furs and jewels, receives her Grammy award.

INT. A PRISON CELL, 1953 — DAY

Close-up of the wall of Barbara's cell in the state pen. We pan across the wall seeing the pencil marks checking off the days of the week. There are twenty sets of six pencil slashes with the seventh going diagonally across. Barbara's hand is seen drawing a diagonal slash across the six slashes indicating week number twenty-one.

EXT. HOLLYWOOD BOULEVARD, 1954 – DAY

Angela, once more surrounded by photographers, is presented with her star on Hollywood Boulevard.

INT. A PRISON CELL, 1953 – DAY

Repeated tight, tighter, and even tighter close-ups of Barbara screaming in agony.

EXT. A STREET IN L.A., 1954 – DAY

Barbara, worn out and bereft, is released from prison and walks down the street carrying her battered suitcase.

Angela's vocal track from the TV show finishes.

EXT. THE BACK OF THE SUSSMAN HOUSE – NIGHT

Back in the present, the two kids stare at their mother. She stumbles and falls to the ground. She crawls through the grass. Edith takes her chiffon scarf and dangles it in front of Barbara, who pushes it away in terror.

> LANCE
> She's really strung out, man.

> EDITH
> Far out.

EXT. OUTSIDE THE SUSSMAN HOME, 1954 – DAY

Barbara, haggard and carrying her suitcase, rings the doorbell. The door opens and we see from Barbara's POV, the glamorous Angela. It's now clear that they are identical twins. Angela looks her bedraggled sister up and down before letting her into the house. As Angela lets her in, she holds her nose from the stench.

INT. THE DEN, 1954 – DAY

Angela and Barbara are seated in the den. The "twins" converse in true *The Patty Duke Show* fashion. Never split screen. We always see one twin's face and the back of the other one's head.

> BARBARA
> Angela, it's so lovely in here. I can smell the roses from your garden.

> ANGELA
> And you reek of the state pen. Blessedly, I haven't seen you for years. What is it you want from me, Barbara?

BARBARA

Want? Oh, I don't know. Perhaps a shoulder to cry on. All these
years since the act broke up, I've never wanted to impose on you.

ANGELA

But now you have.

BARBARA

I'm just so terribly alone. Do you even know what loneliness is?

EXT. THE BACK OF THE SUSSMAN HOUSE – NIGHT

Back in the present, Barbara tries to stand up but Lance trips her and
she falls flat on her face. Sobbing, he kisses her on the cheek. Barbara
tenderly strokes his face.

LANCE

What are you seeing now, bitch, whore, acid-freak?

INT. THE DEN, 1954 – DAY

Barbara continues speaking to Angela.

BARBARA

Angela, you're so very fortunate. A brilliant career, a wonderful
marriage, two perfect children.

ANGELA

My good fortune seems to have ended. My deadbeat sister arrives
at my doorstep a complete and utter failure, expecting a handout.

BARBARA

But, Angela, I never said anything of the kind.

ANGELA

Barbara, we're twins. We can read each other's minds. Well,
perhaps you can make yourself useful.

INT. ANGELA'S BEDROOM, 1954 – NIGHT

Angela and Sol are having a violent fight. He tries to restrain her as
she tries to scratch his face. Through the open bathroom door,
Barbara, on her knees scrubbing the floor, observes them.

INT. THE CHILDREN'S BEDROOM, 1954 – NIGHT

The children (seven and nine) are asleep in their beds. The door swings
open and Angela appears, silhouetted in the light. The children wake
up in terror. Drunk, she swaggers into the room and trips on one of
Lance's dolls lying on the floor. This puts her in an uncontrollable

rage. She twists the head off the doll and hurls it at Lance. She rips the sheets and blankets off the beds leaving the children cowering. She looks around the room and notices the children's pet hamster in its cage. With an evil glint in her eye, she removes the hamster and despite the children's screams, she squeezes the pet until it's dead.

As Angela staggers out of the room, "Aunt" Barbara appears in silhouette in the door frame. Angela shoves Barbara out of the way and exits. "Aunt" Barbara rushes over to the frightened children and holds them close to her.

EXT. THE BACK OF THE SUSSMAN HOUSE – NIGHT

Tight close-up of Barbara.

> BARBARA (V.O.)
> If my sister died, no one would mourn. If my sister died, I would be free. I could be Angela. A better wife, a better mother, a better star!

Under Barbara's voiceover, the past is replayed.

EXT. THE SWIMMING POOL AND PATIO, 1954 – DAY

Barbara carries out a tray of drinks and sees Angela sunbathing on a chaise.

> BARBARA (V.O.)
> The house is empty. The children are away with the governess.

Barbara slips the sleeping pills into Angela's cocktail.

> BARBARA (V.O.) (CONT'D)
> How many will I need? Are these enough?

INT. BARBARA'S BEDROOM, 1954 – DAY

A comatose Angela is sprawled out on the bed. Barbara helps her out of her clothes.

> BARBARA
> Exchange clothes.

INT. BARBARA'S BEDROOM, 1954 – DAY

LATER

Barbara feverishly tries to copy Angela's hairstyle.

A newscaster's VOICE is heard.

NEWSCASTER (V.O.)

Singer Angela Arden's sister was found dead this morning from an overdose of pills. The coroner's report ruled the death a probable suicide.

EXT. THE BACK OF THE SUSSMAN HOUSE – NIGHT

Barbara will now be called "Angela" again. Lance and Edith are nowhere to be seen.

Angela thinks she hears something. The past and present are one.

ANGELA

Sol? Sol? Are you there?

Angela moves toward the house. Coming toward her is a shadowy figure. To her horror, she hallucinates that a badly decomposed Sol has risen from the grave.

She turns to run away from Sol and confronts another grotesque horror: the equally decomposing figure of the dead "Angela." Angela is nearly mute from terror as the two "corpses" move in toward her.

Angela falls to her knees.

ANGELA (CONT'D)

Yes! Yes! I did it! I killed them both!!

Angela writhes on the ground, a quivering, incoherent wreck, reduced to making animalistic grunts and whimpers. Sol and the dead "Angela" have vanished. Lance and Edith stand in their places and stare at her, their questions answered.

EXT. THE FRONT OF THE SUSSMAN HOUSE – DAY

Late afternoon. Tony comes up the walk. Lance and Edith run outside as Tony reaches the door. Edith is holding an audio-tape.

EDITH

Didn't think you'd ever get here.

TONY

Where's your mother?

EDITH

In her bedroom, dressing for the Oscars. Here's the tape. Proof of Mother's crimes.

TONY

What does she remember of last night?

LANCE

Nothing. She thinks it was all a dream.

INT. ANGELA'S BEDROOM – DAY

Angela, beautifully gowned and coiffed, is preparing to go to the
Oscars. As she sprays herself with perfume, she suddenly has an acid
flashback. She hears voices.

VOICES (V.O.)

Sister. Sister. Sister.

The moment passes and she regains her composure.

EXT. OUTSIDE THE SUSSMAN HOUSE – DAY

Edith clings to Tony. Lance is very puzzled.

EDITH

Tony, take me away from here. I've got money now. Stocks,
bonds, a supermarket in West Covina.

She covers his face with kisses. Lance breaks them apart.

LANCE

Hey, I thought I was the one you were hot for.

EDITH

You? You? How's the weather in Fantasyland?

TONY

Now both of you wait just one second.

EDITH

Wait nothing. That eleven-inch dong has my luggage tags on it.

LANCE

Not on your life, Lady Scarface!

Edith knocks Lance to the ground. It escalates into an ugly catfight as
they roll around on the lawn.

EDITH

You'll never have him, Brain Dead!

INT. THE SUSSMAN LIVING ROOM – DAY

From the POV of a hooded intruder, Angela descends the staircase. The
intruder hides behind the window drapery.

Trying to make some sense of the nightmarish events of the previous
night, Angela crosses to the stereo. She finds the record album that

Lance was lip-synching to. Behind her back, the black hooded figure appears from behind a drapery, holding a rope. He throws it around her neck and attempts to strangle her. She manages to release herself from his hold and pull off the black hood. It's Sol!

ANGELA
(in shock)
But you – you're –

SOL
Didn't think a dead man could be so strong?

ANGELA
(pulling herself together)
The cuisine in Hades must be top-notch.

SOL
Actually, it's not bad in Pasadena. That's where I've been holing up.

ANGELA
But I don't understand. I thought –

Sol takes a gun out of his pocket.

SOL
You thought you killed me? Dear loyal Bootsie was onto you. She found that little vial and replaced the poison with baking soda. That was a neat trick you tried to pull with the suppository. Not only didn't it kill me but I'm just as constipated as I was before.

ANGELA
And you played this cruel charade on your own children?

SOL
You should know that your beloved children laced your coffee with LSD. I hid out here last night. You were on some bender.

ANGELA
LSD? So that's what happened. My dream.

SOL
Yes, your dream. Very revealing, BARBARA! You evil bitch! You killed her. You killed your sister. You killed Angela!

Angela, distraught, crosses to the wet-bar and fixes herself a drink to steady her nerves. Sol follows her.

> SOL (CONT'D)

How could you ever think that you could replace her? As a wife perhaps, as a mother, but as a star? Barbara, you were always a no-talent amateur! A loser!

Angela tosses her drink in his face. Sol drops the gun and they scuffle for it. Angela grabs hold of the gun.

> SOL (CONT'D)

You'll go to the gas chamber for this.

Angela is suddenly struck by an essential truth of her strange existence. Still pointing the gun at Sol, she tries to sort things out.

> ANGELA

Yes. And I don't really care. All my life what I feared most was loneliness. That terrible aching kind of loneliness. It's a dark, empty place to live. Somehow, I'm not afraid of that darkness anymore. I'm not afraid.

EXT. OUTSIDE THE SUSSMAN HOME – NIGHT

Tony separates the battling kids.

> TONY

Stop it! Both of you! Guess it's time I revealed the truth about myself. Although a card carrying member of the Screen Actors Guild, I'm also an agent with the FBI. I've been undercover for the past six months.

> LANCE

Undercover? Under the sheets.

> TONY

My father was also with the bureau. He was part of the original investigation into the suicide of Barbara Arden.

INT. BARBARA'S BEDROOM, 1954 – NIGHT

FLASHBACK

Angela's corpse is lying on the bed. A POLICE PHOTOGRAPHER is taking pictures. Tony's father, who looks exactly like his son, is jotting down notes.

> TONY (V.O.)

He was sure that Barbara killed Angela Arden and took her place. Everyone thought he was off his beam. Dad died a broken man.

END OF FLASHBACK

INT. OUTSIDE THE SUSSMAN HOUSE – DAY

Tony looks up at Angela's window.

> TONY
> I've been obsessed with getting to the truth of this mystery, and now you kids have solved it for me.

> EDITH
> But, Tony, you stole my virginity.

> LANCE
> And what about the head to toe tongue bath I gave you?

> TONY
> I'm afraid it was all in the line of duty. I want you both to come with me to the office and officially surrender the tape.

> LANCE
> This isn't quite what I had in mind.

They hear a GUNSHOT and run toward the house.

INT. THE SUSSMAN LIVING ROOM – DAY

Angela's shot has missed Sol and, instead, decapitated a statue.

> SOL
> You crazy tramp, you coulda killed me.

Lance, Edith, and Tony enter through the front door.

> EDITH
> Daddy! You're alive.

> SOL
> My baby.

> TONY
> Mr. Sussman, you have some explaining to do.

> EDITH
> Daddy, no more secrets. Please.

> SOL
> What does it matter now? Cards on the table. I was in deep trouble with the mob. Owed them millions that I could never repay.

INT. SOL'S DEN – DAY

FLASHBACK

Bootsie is seated behind Sol's desk, clearly in charge, going over the details of the plan with Sol.

> SOL (V.O.)
> There was no way out. Until Bootsie made me see that my wife was plotting my murder. That's when she got the idea.

INT. THE KITCHEN – DAY

Bootsie pours baking soda into the vial.

> SOL (V.O.)
> Bootsie's new, improved plan was to make Angela think she really did kill me.

INT. SOL'S BEDROOM – NIGHT

Sol lies "dead" on the floor. Lance comforts Angela. Edith sobs on the bed. Bootsie examines the "corpse," who winks at her.

> SOL
> What if we made everyone believe I died? I could start a brand new life with a new name.

END OF FLASHBACK

INT. THE SUSSMAN LIVING ROOM – EARLY EVENING

Sol continues his tale.

> SOL
> And with the help of a plastic surgeon, a new face.

> EDITH
> But I was there when the police arrived.

> SOL
> Professional actors.

> LANCE
> The ambulance driver?

> SOL
> Professional actor.

> ANGELA
> The coroner?

> SOL
> Community theatre.

EDITH

And you were never going to see me again?

SOL

My plan was to hotfoot it to San Paulo. After the dust settled, I was going to contact you and give you my new identity, Mrs. Hilda Sanchez.

POLICE SIRENS are heard outside.

LANCE

But who killed Bootsie?

SOL

I killed Bootsie.

INT. ANGELA'S BEDROOM – DAY

FLASHBACK

Bootsie hurls Angela's gown to the floor when Sol appears from behind the door and moves menacingly toward her.

END OF FLASHBACK

INT. THE SUSSMAN LIVING ROOM – NIGHT

Sol looks at his murderous hands in disgust.

SOL

She loved me so much. But she was a loose end with a loose mouth. I would never be safe as long as she lived.

TONY

Mr. Sussman, it's time to go.

Tony places Sol's hands in handcuffs.

EDITH

Daddy, I'll write every day.

SOL

The Sussman tradition is in your hands. "Make it big, give it class, leave 'em with a message."

Tony leads Sol outside where they are greeted by a barrage of Paparazzi.

Edith and Lance are peering out of the window, watching the police car pull away. Angela realizes that on this remarkable night, all the ghosts, once and for all, must be banished.

ANGELA

Edie, if you could only believe that behind all the madness, I so
wanted to be your mother.

EDITH

Please, don't.

ANGELA

You always knew I was an imposter, didn't you?

EDITH

I suppose that unconsciously I did. And it left me confused and
angry.

ANGELA

For that I shall never forgive myself. But you, Lance, that darling
little boy who no one cared to understand. This was someone who
needed me. And it felt so good to be needed.

LANCE

I did need you, Mo –

ANGELA

Perhaps you should call me, Auntie Barbara.

LANCE

Mother.

Angela can barely hold back her tears of gratitude.

ANGELA

Thank you.

Lance embraces her.

Like Helen Keller saying "Waa Waa" for the first time, Edith has an
emotional breakthrough by finally speaking the secret language. The
translation is in subtitles.

EDITH

Ni ove pou, Rother. (I love you, Mother.)

ANGELA

You broke the code. I always knew you would.

Angela holds both children in her arms at last.

Tony reenters the house.

TONY

This is so hard for me to say. I've pursued you for years, hoping to trip you up, to force a confession, but in the process, I've become obsessed with you. You're an enchantress. I can't let you go.

ANGELA

But you must. It is your duty.

TONY

I'll say the tape was a hoax. A big joke. Of course, you're Angela. No one could have pulled off such a masquerade. I'll swear this to be true, if Lance and Edith will back me up.

LANCE

Of course, we will. Won't you, Edie?

EDITH

Of course, we will.

ANGELA

For that I am truly grateful. But I mustn't keep my police escort waiting.

LANCE

But Mother, if you turn yourself in, they'll give you the death sentence for sure.

ANGELA
(with radiant serenity)
And yet, by giving myself up, I seek a kind of freedom.

Angela places her wrap around her shoulders.

The two dogs scamper down the stairs and rush about her feet. She kneels down and hugs her beloved twin puppies for perhaps the last time. She's ready to go.

Angela opens the door. There is a wild flashing of cameras. She exits the house.

EXT. OUTSIDE THE SUSSMAN HOME – NIGHT

With great dignity, Angela walks past the crowd of PHOTOGRAPHERS, POLICE, and gawking NEIGHBORS.

Lance and Edith, with tears in their eyes, watch from the doorway. Tony stops Angela just before she reaches the waiting police car.

TONY

I'll go with you. You shouldn't do this alone.

ANGELA

Thank you, Tony. But I won't be alone, not really, because for the first time I have me. And that's a wonderful feeling.

At this moment, Barbara as "Angela" has the true stature of a great star. She rises to the occasion and enters the police car as if it were a royal carriage.

The cameras flash madly as the car proceeds down the street carrying "Angela" to her destiny.

END OF FILM

CREDITS

ANGELA ARDEN/BARBARA ARDEN	Charles Busch
TROY PARKER	Jason Priestley
EDITH SUSSMAN	Natasha Lyonne
BOOTSIE CARP	Frances Conroy
SOL SUSSMAN	Philip Baker Hall
LANCE SUSSMAN	Stark Sands
POLICEMAN	Josh Hutchinson
SAM FISHBEIN	Victor Raider-Wexler
SHATZI VAN ALLEN	Nora Dunn
TUCHMAN	Stanley de Santis
LEATHER DADDY	Paul Vinson

Written by	Charles Busch
Based on the play *Die, Mommie, Die!*	by Charles Busch
Cinematography by	Kelly Evans
Directed by	Mark Rucker
Produced by	Aviator Films
Producer	Dante Di Loreto
Executive Producer	Lonny Dubrofsky
Producer	Anthony Edwards
Associate Producer	Robert Hall
Producer	Bill Kenwright
Co-producer	Frank Pavich
Co-executive Producer	Neil Weinman

Stills

Andrew Levitas stars as "Provoloney" (left) and Nick Cornish stars as "Yo Yo" (right) in Strand Releasing/New Oz and Red Horse Films' *Psycho Beach Party*. Photo credit: Mark Lipson © 1999.

(left to right) Lauren Ambrose stars as "Chicklet," Amy Adams stars as "Marvel Ann," and Danni Wheeler stars as "Berdine" in Strand Releasing/New Oz and Red Horse Films' *Psycho Beach Party*. Photo credit: Mark Lipson © 1999.

(left to right) Lauren Ambrose stars as "Chicklet," Charles Busch stars as "Capt. Monica Stark," and Thomas Gibson stars as "Kanaka" in Strand Releasing/New Oz and Red Horse Films' *Psycho Beach Party*. Photo credit: Mark Lipson © 1999.

Charles Busch stars as "Capt. Monica Stark" (left) and Kimberly Davies stars as "Bettina Barnes" (right) in Strand Releasing/New Oz and Red Horse Films' *Psycho Beach Party*. Photo credit: Mark Lipson © 1999.

Charles Busch as "Angela Arden" in Aviator Films/Sundance Channel Home Entertainment's *Die, Mommie, Die!* Photo credit: Courtesy of the Sundance Channel © 2003.

Charles Busch (center) as "Angela Arden" in Aviator Films/Sundance
Channel Home Entertainment's *Die, Mommie, Die!* Photo credit:
Courtesy of the Sundance Channel © 2003.

Charles Busch (left) as "Angela Arden" and Jason Priestley as "Tony Parker" in Aviator Films/Sundance Channel Home Entertainment's *Die, Mommie, Die!* Photo credit: Courtesy of the Sundance Channel © 2003.

(Left to right) Natasha Lyonne as "Edith Sussman," Frances Conroy as "Bootsie Carp," Stark Sands as "Lance Sussman," and Charles Busch as "Angela Arden" in Aviator Films/Sundance Channel Home Entertainment's *Die, Mommie, Die!* Photo credit: Courtesy of the Sundance Channel © 2003.